EMOTIONALLY
INTELLIGENT
RE

Barnabas
in
Schools

Text copyright © Cavan Wood 2014
The author asserts the moral right
to be identified as the author of this work

Published by
The Bible Reading Fellowship
15 The Chambers, Vineyard
Abingdon OX14 3FE
United Kingdom
Tel: +44 (0)1865 319700
Email: enquiries@brf.org.uk
Website: www.brf.org.uk
BRF is a Registered Charity

ISBN 978 1 84101 617 7

First published 2014
10 9 8 7 6 5 4 3 2 1 0
All rights reserved

Acknowledgements
Unless otherwise stated, scripture quotations are taken from the Contemporary English
Version of the Bible published by HarperCollins Publishers, copyright © 1991, 1992, 1995
American Bible Society.

Scripture quotations taken from the Holy Bible, New International Version (Anglicised edition),
copyright © 1979, 1984,2011 by Biblica. Used by permission of Hodder & Stoughton
Publishers, an Hachette UK company. All rights reserved. 'NIV' is a registered trademark of
Biblica. UK trademark number 1448790.

Scripture quotations from *THE MESSAGE*. Copyright © Eugene H. Peterson 1993, 1994, 1995.
Used by permission of NavPress Publishing.

Every effort has been made to trace and contact copyright owners for material used in this
resource. We apologise for any inadvertent omissions or errors, and would ask those concerned
to contact us so that full acknowledgement can be made in the future.

A catalogue record for this book is available from the British Library

Printed and bound by CPI Group (UK) Ltd, Croydon CR0 4YY

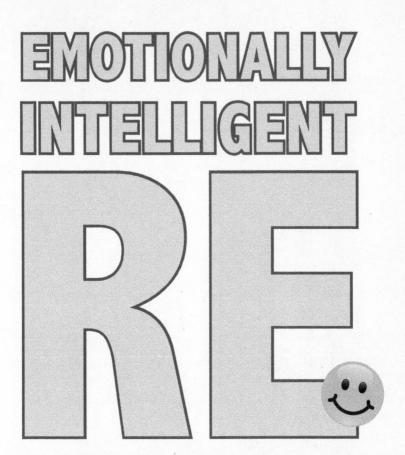

EMOTIONALLY
INTELLIGENT
RE

**Learning about our emotions
from Bible stories**

CAVAN WOOD

Contents

+

Introduction

Why do we teach RE? There have been many different reasons given in the last few decades. In the 1940s and 1950s, it was to help children understand their faith—which was assumed to be Christian. In the 1960s, there was an increasing emphasis on moral problems, and the 1970s and the 1980s saw a desire to pursue multi-faith teaching. By the 1990s, RE was no longer confessional but assumed multi-faith, no faith or some faith. Many people were retreating from the ideas of phenomenology (the study of religion by concentrating on the experiences and rituals that religious believers have) and began to be interested in the philosophy of religion.

With the emphasis on 'learning about' and 'learning from' that developed in the late 1990s, RE teachers began to realise that something needed to be done to make bridges with children who were highly secular in their outlook. Some attention has been paid to emotions and mental states, but I think we need to do more. Self-understanding or 'emotional intelligence'—whichever phrase you use—has never been more urgently needed than today. The ancient Greek oracle at Delphi told people, 'Know yourself', but we can often be far from that knowledge in our world today.

Becoming emotionally healthy

To be a healthy person, there are a number of aspects we need to cultivate.

- **Physical:** We need to be physically fit to enjoy life, with the energy to cope with the demands we face. There needs to be a balance to make sure that we keep our bodies in the shape they should be in.

- **Emotional:** We need the ability to be honest with ourselves about what we are feeling and why. We need to see emotions as important indicators of the way we are, without elevating them to become the only way we interpret reality.
- **Mental:** Every person who is healthy is engaging with the world, thinking through their relationships and their priorities. We may need to have a logical approach to the issues we face.
- **Spiritual:** Everyone needs an approach to life that enables them to see beyond themselves and their immediate situations and relationships. For many people, this will involve following a religion that can help them understand the realities of life and death and the big questions of life.
- **Relational:** We are meant to be social animals, and we need to make relationships with others. The work of the American sociologist Robert Puttnam, in his study *Bowling Alone*, suggests that people who belong to groups are much better able to cope with difficulties and may even live longer than those who have few relationships. Puttnam used the example that many Americans were going to the bowling alley alone rather than taking part in clubs or going with friends.

The psychologist Oliver James believes that many people are not experiencing emotional health. In his book *Affluenza* (Vermilion, 2007), he looks at the way wealth and power can make people miserable, when they should be joyful about having things that could bring them peace. James offers some suggestions for achieving emotional health, which include the following.

- Live in the present: don't obsess about the past. You will begin to experience the enjoyment of the moment.
- Reflect on what you have done and try not to repeat the same mistakes. Go easy on yourself: we all make mistakes, and we need to realise that we will not be able to match the image we would like to have of ourselves.

- Listen and talk to people, seeing each one as valuable. If we communicate this sense of value to others, they will give it back to us, and we will then be helping ourselves to develop the type of relationships that will enable us to deal with the difficulties of life.
- Be playful: don't take life too seriously. There is a time to be serious, but having a sense of humour and fun is an important survival advantage.
- Have a lively approach to life rather than being too busy. Being too busy means that we do not see what is really important; we mistake activity for meaning. There are times when we need to stop and think.
- Be true to the person you are. We need to encourage children to follow the words of Polonius in *Hamlet*, 'Above all, to thyself be true', but also to make sure that they do not hurt others or themselves in the process.

Britain, as a nation, is learning to talk more about emotions. The outpouring of grief after the death of Diana, Princess of Wales, in 1997 heralded a sea-change in our attitude to seeing people cry, but young people are still much more willing to talk about their emotions than older people, and women much more than men. We need to help our pupils to talk about their feelings in a relaxed, non-threatening way that helps them to see the importance of emotions.

At the same time, we must guard against becoming self-indulgent and reducing ourselves to *just* emotional beings. We can communicate in so many ways and at such speed that we do not always think about the consequences. Our pupils live in a world of social media and its influence. An ill-chosen word or phrase on a website can lead to tension and misunderstanding. Children may fail to understand, too, that an emotional reaction posted on a website could have a consequence that lasts a lifetime.

It has been said that emotions should be servants, not masters —or at least not tyrants. Emotional intelligence is not about indulgence but about getting things in the right balance. This is difficult to achieve in our culture, and we may find that this approach is at odds with some of the dominant themes of the time.

The eight intelligences

In 1983, psychologist Howard Gardner questioned the way in which we view intelligence. As well as intellectual intelligence, he suggested, there are seven further intelligences or learning styles:

- **Spatial** learners think in terms of physical space. They are highly aware of their environment. They like to draw, do jigsaw puzzles, read maps and daydream. Drawing or making or storing an image helps them to learn.
- **Bodily-kinesthetic** learners use the body effectively, like a dancer or a surgeon. They have a keen awareness of their body and enjoy movement, touch and making things, using technology. They communicate well through body language and like to be taught through physical activity, hands-on learning and acting out, role-playing or other forms of drama.
- **Musical** learners show sensitivity to rhythm and sound. They love music and are sensitive to sounds in their environments. They may study better with music playing in the background.
- **Interpersonal** learners prioritise understanding and interacting with others. They have many friends and well-developed empathy for others. They can be taught well through group activities or dialogues and dramas.
- **Intrapersonal** learners focus on understanding their own interests and goals. These learners tend to shy away from other people, as they prefer their own company. They are in tune with their inner feelings and have wisdom, intuition and motivation, as well as a strong will, confidence and strong opinions. They like to learn alone.
- **Linguistic** learners enjoy using words effectively. These learners have highly developed auditory skills and often think in words.

They like reading, playing word games and making up poetry or stories. They can be taught by being encouraged to say and see words and to read books with their teacher.

• **Logical-mathematical** learners have reasoning and calculation skills as key strengths. These learners think conceptually and abstractly and are able to see and explore patterns and relationships. They can be taught through logic games, through their own guided investigations or by being encouraged to solve or engage with mysteries. They need to learn and form concepts before they can deal with details.

Gardner believed that these intelligences can be overlapping: people might have more than one, but they are likely to have one that is most dominant, which will be their preferred style of learning.

Emotional intelligence

In 1996, psychologist Daniel Goleman suggested an addition to this list—'emotional intelligence' (although, clearly, the interpersonal and intrapersonal intelligences overlap somewhat with his ideas).

The idea of emotional intelligence is that people work at different levels when dealing with their emotions and those of other people. An emotionally intelligent person thinks about the effect that emotions have on their relationships with others, themselves and, if they are religious, with God.

It is important to understand the causes of the things we feel and to recognise that other people may have different emotions, but it is also important to understand that a person's beliefs will affect the way they handle their emotions. Clearly, a number of children will struggle with the concept of emotional intelligence. They may be on the autistic spectrum, for example, or they may have other significant emotional needs or experiences. We need to deal with these children in a sensitive manner.

Author Brian Draper has suggested that there is also another type of intelligence to be considered—'spiritual intelligence'—

the ability to deal with the questions of existence and its meaning (*Spiritual Intelligence: A new way of being*, Lion Hudson, 2009).

Working with Bible stories

In this book, I use the Bible as a resource for looking at human emotions, encouraging teachers to teach the Bible in a way that presents it as a book about life. In the 1960s, Ronald Goldman attacked immature teaching of the biblical narrative by saying, 'The Bible is not a children's book.' In one sense, he was right. The Bible is not reducible to a collection of stories that might entertain or instruct children. It is a book that reveals what humanity is like in all its glorious and often contradictory nature. It isn't a children's book, but it is about human beings and their struggles with themselves as well as with the divine. If we are looking for a mirror to the various emotional and mental states of humanity, we will find it in the pages of the Bible.

American president Woodrow Wilson said, 'When you read the Bible, you know it is the word of God, because you have found it the key to your own heart, your own happiness and your own duty.' This is not always easy to accept. The writer James Barr described the Bible as 'a bomb of a book': its challenges can blow our world apart, changing the way we see things.

Due care must be taken to handle the material sensitively, taking into account the personal situations of the children you are teaching—for example, in the session on grief. However, if we can help our pupils with issues in their emotional life, we will be doing them a service. If we can help them to see the Bible as a resource to help them deal with these issues, its perceived lack of relevance to their lives may be overcome.

Although I have chosen to use stories and other passages from the Bible, the same approach could be applied to other religions. We must be careful that we do not reduce any passage we use simply to an illustration of the emotion we want to consider. There is a tendency for us to take a passage and make it more logical, more appealing to a secular mind, than we might be wise to do.

Take the story of Noah's ark. This is often made into a worthy parable about the use and abuse of the environment. Yes, that is an element in the story, but so are ideas about judgement, sin and God's power. We need to hold on to a variety of meanings. Speaking at the Greenbelt festival in August 2012, comedian Frank Skinner said that he felt the church was often too keen to downplay the 'weird nature' of some aspects of faith. He particularly meant that it needed to communicate the supernatural nature of the Christian faith. We are selling children short if we do not introduce them to the theological underpinning of the stories; they will not fully understand what they are studying.

I believe that emotional and biblical literacy are not at odds with each other but can enable children to see the Bible as a well from which all can draw water.

A time to stop and think

There is a book on spirituality for children, by Mary Stone, called *Don't Just Do Something, Sit There*. The title makes you think! We are not just to be active but to be thoughtful. A more emotionally intelligent approach may help to develop other aspects of the children we are teaching. 'Be still, and know that I am God,' says the psalmist in the Bible (Psalm 46:10, NIV). Being still is not something that comes easily to us. We need to find time to be still.

Think about this passage from the Gospel of Luke.

The Lord and his disciples were travelling along and came to a village. When they got there, a woman named Martha welcomed him into her home. She had a sister named Mary, who sat down in front of the Lord and was listening to what he said. Martha was worried about all that had to be done. Finally, she went to Jesus and said, 'Lord, doesn't it bother you that my sister has left me to do all the work by myself? Tell her to come and help me!'

The Lord answered, 'Martha, Martha! You are worried and upset about so many things, but only one thing is necessary. Mary has chosen what is best, and it will not be taken away from her.'
LUKE 10:38–42

Martha is the activist, the person who cannot stop doing things. Mary is the one who stops and listens. A balanced person needs a bit of each, of course, but Jesus challenges Martha to think about who she is as well as how Mary is behaving. Jesus can see all the activities that concern Martha and knows that she needs to stop for a few moments.

The topics in this book can be used with your pupils to create an opportunity to stop and reflect. The following approaches may be helpful:

• Circle time: have a discussion based on one of the themes studied. Make sure that everyone gets a chance to speak and be heard.
• Community of enquiry: a group comes together and collects a number of questions that they would like to answer by further reflection.
• Visit a place linked to quietness, such as a local church, where the children can be encouraged to stop and reflect.
• Invite an expert on silence, such as a monk or nun or a member of the Quakers. They could perhaps introduce the idea of silence to the children and help them think about the possible advantages. Be prepared to find that some children may find silence embarrassing or difficult.
• Try a relaxation exercise. You could encourage pupils to think about a peaceful place, such as a place where they have been on holiday or would like to go.

I hope that this resource will enable your pupils to understand themselves better as both emotional and spiritual beings.

LESSON PLANS

✣

What influences our emotions?

Learning objectives

- All pupils will be able to give reasons for the emotions they experience.
- Most pupils will be able to give reasons why emotions are not always trustworthy.
- Some pupils will be able to give reasons for how emotions can be both positive and negative, and consider other ways in which they can gain self-understanding.

Starter

- Write a list of the emotions that you have felt since you got up this morning.
- Compare your list with a partner. Which are the same? Which are different?

Introduction

What influences our emotions? All kinds of things can do so. How much sleep or food or water we have had can make a difference. The weather can make an enormous difference, as rainy or wintry days with little light can make people feel low. (Seasonal Affective Disorder is a condition that causes people to feel low between November and February, due to the lack of light.) Events such as the divorce of parents or the death of a close family member will also affect a person's mood. We may move through many different emotions in one day.

The psychologist Dr Steve Peters advised the Olympic cycling teams during the 2012 Olympics. He has a theory that, in each one of us, there is a part that is like a computer (carefully working out problems), a part that is more 'human' (thinking about others) and a part that he calls 'the chimp', which is where our emotions rule us. When we speak under the control of the chimp, Peters says, we can often do ourselves and others harm.

Emotions can dominate a person's life. Some of them can be positive but some can be very negative. Our emotions can give us good information or they can mislead us. They will also influence us in our struggle to do right. Let's look at the apostle Paul, who struggled in this way.

But I need something more! For if I know the law but still can't keep it, and if the power of sin within me keeps sabotaging my best intentions, I obviously need help! I realise that I don't have what it takes. I can will it, but I can't do it. I decide to do good, but I don't really do it; I decide not to do bad, but then I do it anyway. My decisions, such as they are, don't result in actions. Something has gone wrong deep within me and gets the better of me every time.

It happens so regularly that it's predictable. The moment I decide to do good, sin is there to trip me up. I truly delight in God's commands, but it's pretty obvious that not all of me joins in that delight. Parts of me covertly rebel, and just when I least expect it, they take charge.

I've tried everything and nothing helps. I'm at the end of my rope. Is there no one who can do anything for me? Isn't that the real question?

The answer, thank God, is that Jesus Christ can and does. He acted to set things right in this life of contradictions where I want to serve God with all my heart and mind, but am pulled by the influence of sin to do something totally different.

ROMANS 7:17–25 (THE MESSAGE)

Reflection

Do you recognise this struggle to do right, or do you always find it easy to do the right thing?

☺ Questions and activities

- What influences a person's emotions? Working with a partner, try to come up with six ideas. Write them in full sentences. Which do you think are the most important and why? What is the least important? Explain why.
- Can you always tell what a person is thinking by looking at them? If not, why not? Give reasons for what you think, showing that you have thought about it from more than one point of view.

Emotional intelligence is part of getting to know who we are. Use this test to help you think about what sort of person you are and how you deal with emotions. There are no right or wrong answers.

1. *I am clear about how I feel.*
   Always   Sometimes   Never

2. *I show respect for other people's feelings.*
   Always   Sometimes   Never

3. *There are good excuses for lying.*
   Always   Sometimes   Never

4. *I understand why people feel guilty when they have done something they think is wrong.*
   Always   Sometimes   Never

5. *I tell the truth.*
   Always   Sometimes   Never

6. *I rarely show anger.*
   True   False

7. *I tend to miss what is going on around me.*
   Always   Sometimes   Never

8. *I act according to my feelings.*
   Always   Sometimes   Never

9. *I know what makes other people upset or angry.*
   Always   Sometimes   Never

10. *I can tell when someone is lying.*
    Always   Sometimes   Never

11. *I always admit when I make a mistake.*
    True   False

12. *I feel uncomfortable when people talk about their feelings.*
    Always   Sometimes   Never

13. *I can tell when someone is nervous.*
    Always   Sometimes   Never

14. *I am good at picking up what others are feeling.*
    Always   Sometimes   Never

15. *I don't understand why people hate each other.*
    True   False

Look at the questions you have been asked. Is there anything that has surprised you?

Are there things you would like to change about yourself?

Ask a close friend to answer these questions about you to make sure that you have given the right answers. They probably think better about you than you do!

Do you think that there are other questions that you need to ask about your own emotions or other people's?

Ideas for assembly themes

- Understanding that we are emotional creatures and that emotions can be good and bad.
- Seeing emotions as one source of information about who we are but not revealing the whole picture.

+

Curiosity: Adam and Eve

Learning objectives

- All pupils will be able to explain the idea of curiosity in the story of Adam and Eve.
- Most pupils will be able to talk about the good and bad types of curiosity in the story of Adam and Eve.
- Some pupils will be able to explain how curiosity can be linked to sin.

Starter

- Working with a partner, write some questions that you would like to know the answers to in life.
- How might you go about finding answers to them? Can all the questions be answered?

Introduction

According to an old proverb, 'Curiosity killed the cat'. It means that curiosity can be destructive; it can lead to bad things, to evil. Yet curiosity has helped people to understand the world and even improve it. Without curiosity, there would have been no discoveries of the planets or medicines or other great scientific advances. One scientist, called Kepler, said of his work, 'I was merely thinking God's thoughts after him.' At the start of the 2012 Paralympic Games, the scientist Professor Stephen Hawking ended his introduction with the two words, 'Be curious.'

In the story of Adam and Eve in the garden of Eden, we see one way of looking at evil. The snake in the story is a symbol for evil. Some Christians and Jews go further and say that it is a picture of a being whom they call the devil. The writer of the story wants to communicate the idea that human beings have a choice to do either good or evil.

Being spiritual and thinking creatures, human beings are naturally curious. Is there a way we can know the difference between good and bad curiosity? Let's look at the story of Adam and Eve in the garden of Eden, and see how their curiosity had far-reaching consequences.

The snake was more cunning than any of the other wild animals that the Lord God had made. One day it came to the woman and asked, 'Did God tell you not to eat fruit from any tree in the garden?'

The woman answered, 'God said we could eat fruit from any tree in the garden, except the one in the middle. He told us not to eat fruit from that tree or even to touch it. If we do, we will die.'

'No, you won't!' the snake replied. 'God understands what will happen on the day you eat fruit from that tree. You will see what you have done, and you will know the difference between right and wrong, just as God does.'

The woman stared at the fruit. It looked beautiful and tasty. She wanted the wisdom that it would give her, and she ate some of the fruit. Her husband was there with her, so she gave some to him, and he ate it too. Straight away they saw what they had done, and they realised they were naked. Then they sewed fig leaves together to make something to cover themselves.

Late in the afternoon a breeze began to blow, and the man and woman heard the Lord God walking in the garden. They were frightened and hid behind some trees.

The Lord called out to the man and asked, 'Where are you?'

The man answered, 'I was naked, and when I heard you walking through the garden, I was frightened and hid!'

'How did you know you were naked?' God asked. 'Did you eat any fruit from that tree in the middle of the garden?'

'It was the woman you put here with me,' the man said. 'She gave me some of the fruit, and I ate it.'

The Lord God then asked the woman, 'What have you done?'

'The snake tricked me,' she answered. 'And I ate some of that fruit.'

GENESIS 3:1–13

Reflection

After they have eaten fruit from the tree to satisfy their curiosity, God asks why they did it. Adam blames Eve, and Eve blames the serpent. The snake had tempted Adam and Eve, telling them that they could be like gods, knowing good and evil.

Many people look at this story and say that the snake is a picture of Satan, a devil. One meaning of the word 'Satan' is 'questioner'. 'Did God really say?' is the question he asks Eve.

Adam and Eve's curiosity led to them disobeying the only rule God had given them, and suffering came into the world as a result.

☺ Questions and activities

- What might be the advantages of curiosity? What are the disadvantages?
- Draw an image to show the idea of curiosity.
- 'There will never be a perfect place, as humans are curious and that means they will always make mistakes that will lead them to hurt themselves and others.' What do you think about this? Give reasons for your answers, showing that you have thought about the question from different points of view.
- List five things that you think make the world less than perfect. How many of these could be put right? Which of them cannot be put right? Give reasons for your answers.

- What do you think paradise might look like, if it existed? Give reasons for your answer.
- Complete the activities on the 'Curiosity' wisdom sheet (see page 25).

Ideas for assembly themes

- Curiosity
- Rule-breaking
- Consequences

Wisdom sheet: Curiosity

Look at these ideas on curiosity. Choose one or more and comment on what the person is saying.

An understanding of the natural world and what's in it is a source of not only great curiosity but of great fulfilment.
SIR DAVID ATTENBOROUGH

Curiosity about life in all of its aspects, I think, is still the secret of great creative people.
LEO BURNETT

Curiosity is one of the great secrets of happiness.
BRYANT H. MCGILL

Curiosity will conquer fear even more than bravery will.
JAMES STEPHENS

I have a certain curiosity for life that drives me and propels me forward.
RACHEL MCADAMS

Finish your thoughts by completing this sentence:

- I think that curiosity is…

Reproduced with permission from *Emotionally Intelligent RE* by Cavan Wood (Barnabas in Schools, 2014)

✢

Anger and jealousy: Cain and Abel

Learning objectives

- All pupils will be able to define anger and jealousy.
- Most pupils will be able to describe how anger and jealousy affect people, referring to the story of Cain and Abel.
- Some pupils will be able to comment and reflect on their own feelings of anger and jealousy.

Starter

Working with a partner, think about these questions:

- What do we mean by the word 'jealousy'?
- Can you give examples of when people are jealous of others?

Introduction

Jealousy is defined as 'resentment against a rival, a person enjoying success or advantage, or against another's success or advantage itself'. Jealousy begins when we see someone else being successful or owning an object or having a friendship with others that we would like to have.

The writer William Shakespeare called jealousy 'a green-eyed monster'. He meant that it is an emotion that can get out of control.

Let's read a story of how jealousy destroyed two people's lives.

Adam and Eve had a son. Then Eve said, 'I'll name him Cain because I got him with the help of the Lord.' Later she had another son and named him Abel.

Abel became a sheep farmer, but Cain farmed the land. One

day, Cain gave part of his harvest to the Lord, and Abel also gave an offering to the Lord. He killed the firstborn lamb from one of his sheep and gave the Lord the best parts of it. The Lord was pleased with Abel and his offering, but not with Cain and his offering. This made Cain so angry that he could not hide his feelings.

The Lord said to Cain: 'What's wrong with you? Why do you have such an angry look on your face? If you had done the right thing, you would be smiling. But you did the wrong thing, and now sin is waiting to attack you like a lion. Sin wants to destroy you, but don't let it!'

Cain said to his brother Abel, 'Let's go for a walk.' And when they were out in a field, Cain killed him.

Afterwards the Lord asked Cain, 'Where is Abel?'

'How should I know?' he answered. 'Am I supposed to look after my brother?'

Then the Lord said: 'Why have you done this terrible thing? You killed your own brother, and his blood flowed on to the ground. Now his blood is calling out for me to punish you. And so, I'll put you under a curse. Because you killed Abel and made his blood run out on the ground, you will never be able to farm the land again. If you try to farm the land, it won't produce anything for you. From now on, you'll be without a home, and you'll spend the rest of your life wandering from place to place.'

'This punishment is too hard!' Cain said. 'You're making me leave my home and live far from you. I will have to wander about without a home, and anyone could kill me.'

'No!' the Lord answered. 'Anyone who kills you will be punished seven times worse than I am punishing you.' So the Lord put a mark on Cain to warn everyone not to kill him. But Cain had to go far from the Lord and live in the Land of Wandering, which is east of Eden.

GENESIS 4:1–16

Reflection

Anger is one of the emotions that we often find most difficult to handle, especially if it comes out of jealousy. We cannot always control it and we might feel unhappy if someone sees us expressing it. There are times when anger can be good, such as when a teacher gets angry because they've seen someone being bullied, but being jealous is not a good reason to get angry. Perhaps the worst time we might get jealous is at a birthday or at Christmas, when we think that someone else has received a better present than we have.

In the story of Cain and Abel, jealousy led to murder. Cain's pride was hurt when God told him that Abel's offering was a better sacrifice than his, and he murdered Abel because he could not stand the fact that his brother was considered better than him. When God confronted Cain about the murder and his responsibility to care for Abel, Cain replied, 'Am I supposed to look after my brother?' In other words, he was saying, 'Do I have a responsibility for my brother?' Cain was being sarcastic, but the storyteller wants us to realise that we are, indeed, all responsible for each other.

☺ Questions and activities

- Draw a spider diagram to show why people get jealous.
- Write a poem or story about how someone learns to deal with jealousy.
- Working in groups of four or five, develop a short play about how jealousy affects a family at Christmas.
- Shakespeare calls jealousy 'a green-eyed monster'. What do you think he means? How is this emotion like a monster?
- Complete the activities on the 'Anger and jealousy' wisdom sheet (see page 30).

Ideas for assembly themes

- Dealing with negative emotions
- Working together at school and at home

Wisdom sheet: Anger and jealousy

Look at these ideas on anger and jealousy. Choose one or more and comment on what the person is saying.

Don't waste time on jealousy. Sometimes you're ahead, sometimes behind.
MARY SCHMID

Those people who disagree are proud of themselves, but they don't really know a thing. Their minds are sick, and they like to argue over words. They cause jealousy, disagreements, unkind words, evil suspicions and nasty quarrels.
1 TIMOTHY 6:4–5

But if your heart is full of bitter jealousy and selfishness, don't boast or lie to cover up the truth.
JAMES 3:14

Jealousy is all the fun you think they had.
ERICA JONG

Jealousy is a mental cancer.
B.C. FORBES

As to the green-eyed monster, jealousy… set on him at once and poison him with extra doses of kindness to the person whom he wants to turn you against.
GEORGE PORTER

Never underestimate the power of jealousy to destroy.
OLIVER STONE

Finish your thoughts by completing these sentences:

- I think that anger is…
- There might be times when anger is…
- I feel jealous when…

Reproduced with permission from *Emotionally Intelligent RE* by Cavan Wood (Barnabas in Schools, 2014)

Pride: The tower of Babel

Learning objectives

- All pupils will be able to explain why the tower of Babel story is about pride.
- Most pupils will be able to explain how the tower of Babel story shows the consequences of pride.
- Some pupils will be able to comment on the ideas about God, as well as human pride, in the tower of Babel story.

Starter

- What are you most proud of in your life? What are you least proud of? Write a list with a partner.
- Is pride a good or a bad thing? Give reasons for your answers.

Introduction

The band U2 play a song called 'Pride (In the name of love)', in which they celebrate the lives of Jesus and Martin Luther King. The title is a way of saying that their message is something to feel very positive about. Some people find it an odd title: how can we have pride in love, when pride often leads to the opposite of love, which is hatred?

The word 'pride' can be used in a positive and a negative way. We might have pride in our appearance, wanting to look as good as we can, perhaps at an important event, or we can have pride in the country that we come from.

For many biblical writers, pride is almost always linked with turning our backs on God. These writers believed that our reaction to the mighty God should be humility—a turning to God. The

31

prophets (whom the Israelites believed to be God's spokespeople) often told the countries around Israel—as well as Israel itself—how proud they were, and some of the Bible stories are about the effects of pride. Let's look at an example of one of these stories.

At first everyone spoke the same language, but after some of them moved from the east and settled in Babylonia, they said: 'Let's build a city with a tower that reaches to the sky! We'll use hard bricks and tar instead of stone and mortar. We'll become famous, and we won't be scattered all over the world.'

But when the Lord came down to look at the city and the tower, he said: 'These people are working together because they all speak the same language. This is just the beginning. Soon they will be able to do anything they want. Come on! Let's go down and confuse them by making them speak different languages— then they won't be able to understand each other.'

So the people had to stop building the city, because the Lord confused their language and scattered them all over the earth. That's how the city of Babel got its name.

GENESIS 11:1–9

Reflection

The story of the tower of Babel was inspired by the real-life struggle between Israel and the city of Babylon. The name 'Babel' can mean 'speaking wildly', but it was also the nickname for the city. The Babylonians built a stepped pyramid temple called a ziggurat, which had on its top a place of worship. They thought that, by building this high tower, they could reach up to the gods themselves. They believed that their temple was a stairway to heaven.

The story mocks this idea. The people of Babel think that they are cleverer than God, so the languages are mixed up across the world to show that God alone is in control. The pride of humanity has led them to be more divided and less in control.

Pride has often led to a breakdown between people of different races and cultures. People may have to overcome pride to help build a new society. Until the 1990s, the country of South Africa was separated along racial lines, with the white people ruling the country and making sure that the black people (who were the majority) did not have power. Things changed in 1990 when Nelson Mandela, a black political leader who had been in prison for nearly 30 years, was released. He could have chosen, when he was set free, to be proud and hurt those who had hurt him, but he decided instead that he wanted South Africa to be a good place. To show this intention, in 1994, he invited the prison guard who had locked him up each night to the ceremony at which he would be inaugurated as president, and put him in a place of honour. Mandela chose kindness over pride. How do you think you would have reacted?

☺ Questions and activities

- In what ways might pride be a good thing? When might pride be a bad thing? What might people be ashamed about, rather than proud?
- Find out more about Nelson Mandela and how he tried to overcome divisions in South Africa.
- Research the Babylonian empire. What did the Babylonians contribute to history?
- Find the words 'patriotism' and 'jingoism' in a dictionary. Explain the difference between them.
- Complete the activities on the 'Pride' wisdom sheet (see page 35).

Ideas for assembly themes

- Pride—good and bad
- Patriotism and jingoism
- Use and abuse of technology
- Self-confidence

Wisdom sheet: Pride

Look at these ideas on pride. Choose one or more and comment on what the person is saying.

What have you done today to make yourself proud?
HEATHER SMALL, 'PROUD'

Anger is the enemy of non-violence and pride is a monster that swallows it up.
MAHATMA GANDHI

Great champions have an enormous sense of pride. The people who excel are those who are driven to show the world and prove… just how good they are.
NANCY LOPEZ

I look upon pride as a sin.
TOMMY LEE JONES

Pride is at the bottom of all great mistakes.
JOHN RUSKIN

A proud man is always looking down on things and people; and of course as long as you're looking down, you can't see something that's above you.
C.S. LEWIS

Finish your thoughts by completing these sentences:

- I think that pride is right when…
- I think pride is wrong when…
- On balance, pride is a…

Reproduced with permission from *Emotionally Intelligent RE* by Cavan Wood (Barnabas in Schools, 2014)

✤

Trust: Abraham and Sarah

Learning objectives

- All pupils will be able to explain how the story of Abraham and Sarah shows the idea of trust.
- Most pupils will be able to explain why trust is important in relationships.
- Some pupils will be able to examine what makes for trust in relationships and what might hinder the growth of trust.

Starter

- How do you know if someone is trustworthy?
- Working with a partner, list the qualities that might show if a person is someone you can trust.

Introduction

How do you know who to trust and who not to trust? Trust is something that builds over time: it is easier to trust a family member or a friend than someone you have just met.

Imagine that you were to leave the home you had lived in for over 50 years. Abraham (originally called Abram) and his wife Sarah left their home for a distant land because Abraham believed that God had spoken to him.

Later the Lord spoke to Abram in a vision, 'Abram, don't be afraid! I will protect you and reward you greatly.'

But Abram answered, 'Lord All-Powerful, you have given me everything I could ask for, except children. And when I die, Eliezer of Damascus will get all I own. You have not given me any

36

children, and this servant of mine will inherit everything.'

The Lord replied, 'No, he won't! You will have a son of your own, and everything you have will be his.' Then the Lord took Abram outside and said, 'Look at the sky and see if you can count the stars. That's how many descendants you will have.' Abram believed the Lord, and the Lord was pleased with him.

GENESIS 15:1–6

Reflection

Learning to trust someone can be difficult. There is a story of a tightrope walker known as Blondin, who set his rope across Niagara Falls and invited people to get into a wheelbarrow and let him push them across the big divide. No one was prepared to do it at first—but then one person volunteered and both of them got safely across. They trusted each other and it worked.

Abram and Sarai (as they were originally called) were asked to do some amazing things. They were old and settled in their town, but then, they believed, God spoke to Abram, asking him to move a thousand miles away, with his family, to a country they had never been to. God was asking them to leave behind a comfortable life and go to one that would have seemed much more difficult. Yet they went, taking their extended family and animals and giving up their former way of life. There would be many mistakes on the way, and many times when they did not show trust in the God who, they believed, had caused them to move in the first place.

There are times when we need to learn to trust ourselves and others. When we are learning to swim, we have to trust that when we kick off from the floor of the swimming pool, we will be supported by the water. We have to trust that we will learn to balance when we first ride a bike. We might well begin with the support of someone else, but there comes a time when we have to let go and trust in ourselves.

When we make a friendship, one of the ways that we test

whether it is a long-term relationship is to trust the person with information we need to share with someone, and see if they keep it to themselves. Trusting can be very difficult, but, when we find someone we can trust, it makes life a lot easier.

😃 Questions and activities

- What qualities make someone trustworthy? How many of these qualities do you think you have?
- Why might some people find it difficult to trust God?
- Do you think that you could have behaved in the same way as Abram?
- Write a job advert for someone who will have a responsible position, such as a teacher or a doctor, where lots of trust will be required.
- Draw an image to show the idea of trust and why it is so important.
- Complete the activities on the 'Trust' wisdom sheet (see page 39).

Ideas for assembly themes

- What makes you trustworthy?
- The importance of personal safety (for example, only travelling with people you know and trust)
- Planning for the future
- Honesty

Wisdom sheet: Trust

Look at these ideas on trust. Choose one or more and comment on what the person is saying.

Love all, trust a few, do wrong to none.
WILLIAM SHAKESPEARE

The best way to find out if you can trust somebody is to trust them.
ERNEST HEMINGWAY

I trust no one, not even myself.
JOSEPH STALIN

Do not let your hearts be troubled. Trust in God; trust also in me.
JESUS (JOHN 14:1, NIV)

Those who trust us educate us.
GEORGE ELIOT

Trust is a treasured item and relationship. Once it is tarnished, it is hard to restore its original glow.
WILLIAM WARD

Trust is the glue of life. It's the most essential ingredient in effective communication. It's the foundational principle that holds all relationships.
STEPHEN R. COVEY

Finish your thoughts by completing these sentences:

- I think that trust is...
- I find it easy/difficult to trust because...
- I think I am/am not trustworthy because...
- Sometimes, trust is...

Reproduced with permission from *Emotionally Intelligent RE* by Cavan Wood (Barnabas in Schools, 2014)

✢

Guilt: Joseph and his brothers

Learning objectives

- All pupils will be able to explain the idea of guilt, referring to the story of Joseph.
- Most pupils will be able to talk about their own experiences of guilt.
- Some pupils will be able to reflect on necessary and unnecessary guilt.

Starter

Look at this list of things you might do:

- Lying to a friend
- Being rude to a teacher
- Being nasty to a friend

How would you feel if you had done any of these things? How might you deal with each of these situations? Discuss with a partner.

Introduction

Knowing that you have done wrong and hurt someone else might lead to feelings of guilt. Guilt is the emotion of regret because you could have done something better or avoided doing something bad. It is the feeling of wishing that you had not made a mistake.

Sometimes guilt is the right response to the realisation that we have done something wrong, but sometimes we feel guilty when we have not done anything wrong.

How do you deal with this emotion?

Let's take a look at the biblical story of Joseph, which is found in Genesis 37—50. A shortened version is printed below.

Joseph was the youngest of the sons of Jacob. As the youngest, he became quite spoilt, and his father gave him a special coat. Joseph often told his brothers how important he was, and they got more and more annoyed with him. One day, they decided that enough was enough. They took Joseph and threw him down a well. A group of traders from the country of Midian then came past, and Joseph's brothers sold him as a slave.

When the brothers returned home, they took Joseph's special coat, stained with the blood of a goat that they had killed for the purpose. They showed it to their father and told him that Joseph was dead. Jacob was griefstricken. For years on end, the brothers kept up the lie that their brother had died.

Meanwhile, Joseph had been sold to an Egyptian official called Potiphar. His wife found Joseph attractive and, when he refused to kiss her, she had him arrested, saying he had tried to attack her.

While he was in prison, Joseph became friendly with two men who had served the king of Egypt, known as the Pharaoh. He was able to explain their dreams. The Pharaoh heard about this gift and asked him to explain two dreams that he had had. Joseph told him that the dreams meant there would be seven years of great harvests, followed by seven poor harvests, so Egypt needed to prepare for the time of famine. The Pharaoh was so impressed that he gave Joseph the job of organising the food stores and made him Prime Minister.

Joseph's family in Israel suffered during the famine and the brothers went to Egypt twice to buy food there. The second time, they took with them Joseph's younger brother, Benjamin. Joseph met his brothers, but it had been so many years since they had last seen him that they did not recognise him.

When Joseph talked to them, they told him about their brother who had 'died'. Joseph decided that he needed to make them think about what they had done, so he arranged for the youngest brother, Benjamin, to have a silver cup planted in the sack of food that he was given to carry home. Joseph then accused him of stealing and insisted that he stay in Egypt as his slave. The brothers were guilt-stricken, realising that the loss of Benjamin would break their father's heart.

When he saw how guilty the brothers felt, Joseph could no longer conceal who he really was. When the brothers realised that he was the brother they had lied about and sold to slave traders, but that he was now the second most powerful man in Egypt, they felt guilty about what they had done and were afraid of what might happen to them.

Joseph decided that he wanted to forgive them for what they had done. The guilt of the previous years had gone: this was a time for a new start and forgiveness.

😃 Questions and activities

- How do you think you would have reacted to the brothers if you had been Joseph?
- What sort of things make you feel guilty? Are you always right to feel like this?
- Devise a drama on the theme of guilt.
- Design a collage to show the story of Joseph and his brothers.
- 'Guilt is a good thing, as it proves that our consciences are working.' What do you think? Do you agree? Give reasons for your answer, showing that you have thought about it from more than one point of view.
- Complete the activities on the 'Guilt' wisdom sheet (see page 44).

Ideas for assembly themes

- Guilt
- Learning to say 'sorry'
- Rebuilding broken relationships
- Responsibility

Wisdom sheet: Guilt

Look at these ideas about guilt. Choose one or more and comment on what the person is saying.

I don't believe in guilt, I believe in living on impulse as long as you never intentionally hurt another person, and don't judge people in your life. I think you should live completely free.
ANGELINA JOLIE

Nothing is more wretched than the mind of a man conscious of guilt.
PLUTARCH

I don't feel guilt. Whatever I wish to do, I do.
JEANNE MOREAU

Repentant tears wash out the stain of guilt.
AUGUSTINE OF HIPPO

A guilty conscience needs no accuser.
ENGLISH PROVERB

Every person is guilty of all the good that they didn't do.
VOLTAIRE

Finish your thoughts by completing these sentences:

- I am a person who feels guilt/does not feel guilt...
- I think a person should feel guilty when...

Fear: Moses at the burning bush

Learning objectives

- All pupils will be able to explain what fear is and what might cause it.
- Most pupils will be able to explain how fear can be overcome, with reference to the story of Moses at the burning bush.
- Some pupils will be able to explain how fear can be both a positive and a negative aspect of human experience, and will be able to analyse the story of Moses at the burning bush.

Starter

- What things are people are afraid of? Try to write or draw as many different things as you can.
- Share your ideas with a partner.

Introduction

American president Franklin D. Roosevelt once said, 'We have nothing to fear but fear itself.' Some people are so gripped by fear that they have what is called a phobia. Examples of phobias are claustrophobia (a fear of small, enclosed spaces) and agoraphobia (a fear of wide open spaces). Other people might have a fear of heights. Sometimes these fears start with a bad experience. Some people try to be cured of their fears; other people try to live their lives avoiding them. How do you deal with the fears that you have?

Can the emotion of fear sometimes be a good thing? In the film *Fearless*, the lead character loses all his fear when he survives a plane crash. He then begins to take more and more risks, which threaten himself and others. The film suggests that we need some fears. For example, a person who drives a car without any fear of hurting others will probably not be driving as carefully as they should.

The people of the Bible believed that fear of God was necessary: it was a respect for him that meant people did not treat him lightly. In the following story, we find out that Moses had a fear of God.

One day, Moses was taking care of the sheep and goats of his father-in-law Jethro, the priest of Midian, and Moses decided to lead them across the desert to Sinai, the holy mountain. There an angel of the Lord appeared to him from a burning bush. Moses saw that the bush was on fire, but it was not burning up. 'This is strange!' he said to himself. 'I'll go over and see why the bush isn't burning up.'

When the Lord saw Moses coming near the bush, he called him by name, and Moses answered, 'Here I am.'

God replied, 'Don't come any closer. Take off your sandals—the ground where you are standing is holy. I am the God who was worshipped by your ancestors Abraham, Isaac, and Jacob.'

Moses was afraid to look at God, and so he hid his face.

The Lord said: 'I have seen how my people are suffering as slaves in Egypt, and I have heard them beg for my help because of the way they are being ill-treated. I feel sorry for them, and I have come down to rescue them from the Egyptians.

'I will bring my people out of Egypt into a country where there is good land, rich with milk and honey. I will give them the land where the Canaanites, Hittites, Amorites, Perizzites, Hivites, and Jebusites now live. My people have begged for my help, and I have seen how cruel the Egyptians are to them. Now go to the king! I am sending you to lead my people out of his country.'

But Moses said, 'Who am I to go to the king and lead your people out of Egypt?'

God replied, 'I will be with you. And you will know that I am the one who sent you, when you worship me on this mountain after you have led my people out of Egypt.'

Moses answered, 'I will tell the people of Israel that the God their ancestors worshipped has sent me to them. But what should I say, if they ask me your name?'

God said to Moses: 'I am the eternal God. So tell them that the Lord, whose name is "I Am", has sent you. This is my name for ever, and it is the name that people must use from now on.'
EXODUS 3:1–15

Reflection

Writer Rudolf Otto, in his book *The Idea of the Holy*, said that holiness is both attractive and frightening. It is attractive to believe in a being who is better than humans, yet this is also a very scary thing, as such a holy, perfect God is far removed from the way humans behave. We can be attracted to things we feel afraid of, such as a film or television series that might shock us, or a book about ghosts that might scare us. Some of us might enjoy going on scary rides at adventure parks.

☺ Questions and activities

- Write a version of the story of the burning bush from Moses' point of view, trying to describe why it was an important moment in his life.
- Are there some good fears? Give reasons for your answers.
- 'A God who makes people feel afraid isn't a very good God.' What do you think? Give reasons for your answer, showing that you have thought about it from more than one point of view.
- Write a poem about fear.
- Complete the activities on the 'Fear' wisdom sheet (see page 49).

Ideas for assembly themes

- How to deal with fear
- How to help others deal with fear

Wisdom sheet: Fear

Look at these ideas on fear. Choose one or more and comment on what the person is saying.

Perfect love drives out fear.
1 JOHN 4:18 (NIV)

Fear has its use but cowardice has none.
MAHATMA GANDHI

In order to succeed, your desire for success should be greater than your fear of failure.
BILL COSBY

The fear of death follows from the fear of life. A man who lives fully is prepared to die at any time.
MARK TWAIN

People always fear change. People feared electricity when it was invented, didn't they? People feared coal; they feared gas-powered engines... There will always be ignorance, and ignorance leads to fear.
BILL GATES

Keep your fears to yourself; share your courage with others.
ROBERT LOUIS STEVENSON

Finish your thoughts by completing these sentences:

- I think that fear is...
- The fears that I have are...
- I think I can/can't overcome these fears because...

Reproduced with permission from *Emotionally Intelligent RE* by Cavan Wood (Barnabas in Schools, 2014)

✛

Loyalty: Ruth and Naomi

Learning objectives

- All pupils will be able to explain the idea of loyalty with reference to the story of Ruth and Naomi.
- Most pupils will be able to explain some of the problems that loyalty might cause.
- Some pupils will be able to give a developed opinion on the pros and cons of being loyal.

Starter

- What does the idea of loyalty mean? Do you think that you are a loyal person?
- Share your ideas with a partner.

Introduction

Being loyal is a very important quality. If someone is in the armed forces, they need to be loyal to the country they are fighting for. Friends should be loyal to each other, staying close when things get tough. For some people, loyalty needs to be earned: a person or country should show that they deserve it. Others believe that loyalty is a respect that we should show to people, regardless of whether or not they deserve it.

In the story below, we have an example of someone who showed more loyalty than was to be expected.

Before Israel was ruled by kings, Elimelech from the tribe of Ephrath lived in the town of Bethlehem. His wife was named Naomi, and their two sons were Mahlon and Chilion. But when their crops failed, they moved to the country of Moab. And while they were there, Elimelech died, leaving Naomi with only her two sons.

Later, Naomi's sons married Moabite women. One was named Orpah and the other Ruth. About ten years later, Mahlon and Chilion also died. Now Naomi had no husband or sons.

When Naomi heard that the Lord had given his people a good harvest, she and her two daughters-in-law got ready to leave Moab and go to Judah.

As they were on their way there, Naomi said to them, 'Don't you want to go back home to your own mothers? You were kind to my husband and sons, and you have always been kind to me. I pray that the Lord will be just as kind to you. May he give each of you another husband and a home of your own.'

Naomi kissed them. They cried and said, 'We want to go with you and live among your people.'

But she replied, 'My daughters, why don't you return home? What good will it do you to go with me? Do you think I could have more sons for you to marry? You must go back home, because I am too old to marry again. Even if I got married tonight and later had more sons, would you wait for them to become old enough to marry? No, my daughters! Life is harder for me than it is for you, because the Lord has turned against me.'

They cried again. Orpah kissed her mother-in-law goodbye, but Ruth held on to her. Naomi then said to Ruth, 'Look, your sister-in-law is going back to her people and to her gods! Why don't you go with her?'

Ruth answered, 'Please don't tell me to leave you and return home! I will go where you go, I will live where you live; your people will be my people, your God will be my God. I will die where you die and be buried beside you. May the Lord punish me if we are ever separated, even by death!'

When Naomi saw that Ruth had made up her mind to go with her, she stopped urging her to go back.

RUTH 1:1–18

Reflection

Ruth left her country and her religion to stay with her mother-in-law. She did not need to do this, but her relationship with Naomi was based on loyalty. Going to Israel with Naomi meant that she risked becoming poor, having a difficult life and dying without ever having a new husband. Yet what mattered most to Ruth was the care of her relative and friend. She gives us a picture of what it is like to be unselfish—to think first of the needs of others.

☺ Questions and activities

- How might a football fan show their loyalty to their team? How might you show loyalty to a team that you play for?
- How could you show loyalty to your family?
- What does 'blind loyalty' mean? Should you try to demonstrate this or not?
- Write a teaser for the story of Ruth that you could print on the back of a book about her.
- What questions would you like to ask Ruth and Naomi about the story that we have read?
- Complete the activities on the 'Loyalty' wisdom sheet (see page 53).

Ideas for assembly themes

- Commitment to others (to a school team or the school itself)
- Loyalty
- Safeguarding: when is it right to speak about someone's problem?

Wisdom sheet: Loyalty

Look at these ideas on loyalty. Choose one or more and comment on what the person is saying.

A person who deserves my loyalty receives it.
JOYCE MAYNARD

Success is the result of perfection, hard work, learning from failure, loyalty and persistence.
COLIN POWELL

It is better to be faithful than to be famous.
THEODORE ROOSEVELT

Loyalty is the holiest good in the human heart.
SENECA

The strength of a family, like the strength of an army, is in its loyalty to each other.
MARIO PUZO

Finish your thoughts by completing these sentences:

- I think that loyalty is…
- If people are not loyal to each other, I believe…

Reproduced with permission from *Emotionally Intelligent RE* by Cavan Wood (Barnabas in Schools, 2014)

Fear of failure: Hannah

Starter

- Many people are afraid of failure. They might try to do everything to avoid accepting that they have failed.
- Working with a partner, write a list of areas in life where people might have worries about failure.

Introduction

The fear of failure is one of the biggest worries we face, yet every human being will fail at some point. Olympic gold medal winners have days when they lose races. What matters is not that we fail: we will all do that. What matters is how we deal with failure, allowing it to either break or make us.

In *The Limpopo Academy of Private Detection* by Alexander McCall Smith, we have an example of someone who feels like a failure but isn't. Precious Ramotswe is a detective in Botswana, Africa. She has always used a book called *The Principles of Private Detection* by a man called Clovis Anderson, and she believes that he is a genius. Then Clovis arrives in Botswana.

The book that Precious thinks is so important is not a big seller and, in the USA, where Clovis comes from, his detective agency is not successful. He feels a failure, but Precious shows him that his ideas have helped her to solve crimes. She reminds him that there is a great deal to be grateful for in life and that he is not a failure. The fact is that sometimes we can feel a failure when we are not: our emotions don't always get it right.

In the story below, Hannah had not had children and was afraid that she never would. At that time it was common for a man to have more than one wife, and Hannah had to keep on facing her husband's other wife, who made her feel bad about not being able to have children. However, Hannah decided not to worry about it any more but to pray to God.

Elkanah had two wives, Hannah and Peninnah. Although Peninnah had children, Hannah did not have any.

Once a year Elkanah travelled from his home town to Shiloh, where he worshipped the Lord All-Powerful and offered sacrifices. Eli was the Lord's priest there, and his two sons Hophni and Phinehas served with him as priests.

Whenever Elkanah offered a sacrifice, he gave some of the meat to Peninnah and some to each of her sons and daughters. But he gave Hannah even more, because he loved Hannah very much, even though the Lord had kept her from having children of her own.

Peninnah liked to make Hannah feel miserable about not having any children, especially when the family went to the house of the Lord each year.

One day, Elkanah was there offering a sacrifice, when Hannah began crying and refused to eat. So Elkanah asked, 'Hannah, why are you crying? Why won't you eat? Why do you feel so bad? Don't I mean more to you than ten sons?'

When the sacrifice had been offered, and they had eaten the meal, Hannah got up and went to pray. Eli was sitting in his chair near the door to the place of worship. Hannah was brokenhearted and was crying as she prayed, 'Lord All-Powerful, I am your servant, but I am so miserable! Please let me have a son. I will give him to you for as long as he lives, and his hair will never be cut.'

Hannah prayed silently to the Lord for a long time. But her lips were moving, and Eli thought she was drunk. 'How long are you going to stay drunk?' he asked. 'Sober up!'

'Sir, please don't think I'm no good!' Hannah answered. 'I'm not drunk, and I haven't been drinking. But I do feel miserable and terribly upset. I've been praying all this time, telling the Lord about my problems.'

Eli replied, 'You may go home now and stop worrying. I'm sure the God of Israel will answer your prayer.'

'Sir, thank you for being so kind to me,' Hannah said. Then she left, and after eating something, she felt much better.

1 SAMUEL 1:2–18

Reflection

Hannah became pregnant soon after she had prayed. Prayers are not always answered in the way we want, religious people say, but on this occasion they were. When we feel a failure, it does not mean that we are one. Even if we have had a failure, it should not defeat us: it could be the start of helping us to become someone new.

☺ Questions and activities

- Was Hannah right to think that she was a failure?
- Research the life of a successful athlete. Does their story contain any clues as to how we can cope with our natural worry about failing?

- 'We all will fail. What matters is learning from failure.' What does this mean? How could you put it into practice?
- Write a story that shows how failure can lead to success.
- Complete the activities on the 'Fear of failure' wisdom sheet (see page 58).

Ideas for assembly themes

- What we can learn from failure
- Success
- Self-image

Wisdom sheet: Fear of failure

Look at these ideas on failure. Choose one or more and comment on what the person is saying.

Success consists of going from failure to failure without loss of enthusiasm.
WINSTON CHURCHILL

I can accept failure; everyone fails at something. But I can't accept not trying.
MICHAEL JORDAN

Develop success from failures. Discouragement and failure are two of the surest stepping stones to success.
DALE CARNEGIE

Failure is simply the opportunity to begin again, this time more intelligently.
HENRY FORD

Failure means a stripping away of the inessential.
J.K. ROWLING

Show me a thoroughly satisfied man and I will show you a failure.
THOMAS EDISON

A failure is a man who has blundered but is not able to cash in on the experience.
ELBERT HUBBARD

Finish your thoughts by completing these sentences:

- I think that failure is…
- My worst failure was…
- Failure can teach me that…

Reproduced with permission from *Emotionally Intelligent RE* by Cavan Wood (Barnabas in Schools, 2014)

+

Friendship: David and Jonathan

Learning objectives

- All pupils will be able to explain the idea of friendship with reference to the story of David and Jonathan.
- Most pupils will be able to explain the positive and negative aspects of friendship.
- Some pupils will be able to explain how they can solve problems in friendships.

Starter

- 'A friend is a person who will stand by you when things get tough.' How can a friend help you when things are difficult?
- Draw a spider diagram, working with a partner.

Introduction

Everyone needs friends who they can have a laugh with, who they can share their interests with, and who will give them support when life gets difficult.

How did our friendships start? Sometimes, we cannot remember: they are relationships that have grown and deepened over time. Sometimes a friendship begins as we help people to feel valued, perhaps by asking them to an important event in our lives, such as a birthday party.

Friends are people who might share interests with us or have a similar sense of humour. As the friendship develops, we begin to care for each other.

In the story of David and Jonathan, we have a tale of two

friends under pressure. Jonathan was the son of King Saul, whose mental illness made him perceive David as a threat to his rule. Jonathan was torn between being loyal to his father and helping his friend.

David escaped from Prophets Village. Then he ran to see Jonathan and asked, 'Why does your father Saul want to kill me? What have I done wrong?'

'My father can't be trying to kill you! He never does anything without telling me about it. Why would he hide this from me? It can't be true!'

'Jonathan, I swear it's true! But your father knows how much you like me, and he didn't want to break your heart. That's why he didn't tell you. I swear by the Lord and by your own life that I'm only one step ahead of death.'

Then Jonathan said, 'Tell me what to do, and I'll do it.'

David answered: 'Tomorrow is the New Moon Festival, and I'm supposed to have dinner with your father. But instead, I'll hide in a field until the evening of the next day. If Saul wonders where I am, tell him, "David asked me to let him go to his home town of Bethlehem, so he could take part in a sacrifice his family makes there every year."

'If your father says it's all right, then I'm safe. But if he gets angry, you'll know he wants to harm me. Be kind to me. After all, it was your idea to promise the Lord that we would always be loyal friends. If I've done anything wrong, kill me yourself, but don't hand me over to your father.'

'Don't worry,' Jonathan said. 'If I find out that my father wants to kill you, I'll certainly let you know.'

'How will you do that?' David asked.

'Let's go out to this field, and I'll tell you,' Jonathan answered.

When they got there, Jonathan said: 'I swear by the Lord God of Israel, that two days from now I'll know what my father is planning. Of course I'll let you know if he's friendly toward you.

But if he wants to harm you, I promise to tell you and help you escape. And I ask the Lord to punish me severely if I don't keep my promise.'

1 SAMUEL 20:1–13

Reflection

The story shows us that friendship can be difficult when it meets opposition. David remained Jonathan's friend, but when Jonathan's father Saul plunged the country into civil war, it caused Jonathan's death. When Jonathan died, David wrote a poem to express his grief. Friendship can be difficult but it is really important, as it helps us to deal with the complications of life.

☺ Questions and activities

- How did Jonathan show friendship to David?
- Write three questions from the story, with a multiple choice element. For example: 'David was Jonathan's (a) Friend; (b) Brother; (c) Father.'
- Draw an image to show the idea of friendship.
- Write an advert to encourage people to think about the qualities that really good friends should have.
- Complete the activities on the 'Friendship' wisdom sheet (see page 62).

Ideas for assembly themes

- What makes a good friend?
- Peer pressure
- Relationships
- Bullying

Wisdom sheet: Friendship

Look at these ideas on friendship. Choose one or more and comment on what the person is saying.

Friendship is unnecessary, like philosophy, like art... It has no survival value; rather it is one of those things that give value to survival.
C.S. LEWIS

When we honestly ask ourselves which person in our lives means the most to us, we often find that it is those who, instead of giving advice, solutions or cures, have chosen rather to share our pain and touch our wounds with a warm and tender hand.
HENRI NOUWEN

The most I can do for my friend is simply be his friend.
HENRY DAVID THOREAU

The friend is the man who knows all about you, and still likes you.
ELBERT HUBBARD

True friendship should never conceal what it thinks.
ST JEROME

No one can develop freely in this world and find a full life without feeling understood by at least one person.
PAUL TOURNIER

Wishing to be friends is quick work, but friendship is a slow-ripening fruit.
ARISTOTLE

Finish your thoughts by completing these sentences:

- I think that friendship is...
- I think that I am a good/bad friend because...
- One way to make myself a better friend is to...

Reproduced with permission from *Emotionally Intelligent RE* by Cavan Wood (Barnabas in Schools, 2014)

＋

Courage: David and Goliath

Learning objectives

- All pupils will be able to explain courage in the story of David and Goliath.
- Most pupils will be able to explain how the story of David and Goliath might be an example of courage, and how we might show courage in our own lives.
- Some pupils will be able to give some consideration to the limits of courage.

Starter

- What does it mean to be brave and to show courage?
- Discuss this with a partner.

Introduction

In the 19th century, the writer Stephen Crane wrote a book called *The Red Badge of Courage*. The title referred to the idea that every soldier, to show their bravery, needed to have a little wound, a 'red badge', where blood had flowed due to a cut or gunshot. Many people today want to be known as brave and go out of their way to make sure that other people know their attempts to show bravery.

How can you tell the difference between bravery and cowardice? The brave person will often be thinking about someone else as well as themselves, seeing that the other person needs support or encouragement or even rescue from a difficult situation. To be brave might also involve taking the risk of being misunderstood, hurt or somehow not treated as we should be.

Being brave might not be about fighting in a war. It might be facing up to a difficult situation rather than running away. A person who faces an illness that might kill them is often brave. They can end up thinking more about other people than themselves.

Goliath came towards David, walking behind the soldier who was carrying his shield. When Goliath saw that David was just a healthy, good-looking boy, he made fun of him. 'Do you think I'm a dog?' Goliath asked. 'Is that why you've come after me with a stick?' He cursed David in the name of the Philistine gods and shouted, 'Come on! When I'm finished with you, I'll feed you to the birds and wild animals!'

David answered: 'You've come out to fight me with a sword and a spear and a dagger. But I've come out to fight you in the name of the Lord All-Powerful. He is the God of Israel's army, and you have insulted him too!

'Today the Lord will help me defeat you. I'll knock you down and cut off your head, and I'll feed the bodies of the other Philistine soldiers to the birds and wild animals. Then the whole world will know that Israel has a real God. Everybody here will see that the Lord doesn't need swords or spears to save his people. The Lord always wins his battles, and he will help us defeat you.'

When Goliath started forward, David ran towards him. He put a stone in his sling and swung the sling around by its straps. When he let go of one strap, the stone flew out and hit Goliath on the forehead. It cracked his skull, and he fell face down on the ground. David defeated Goliath with a sling and a stone. He killed him without even using a sword.

1 SAMUEL 17:41–50

Reflection

David was just a poor shepherd who took the risk of fighting the giant Goliath when all the Israelite soldiers were afraid. David believed that he could defeat Goliath because God was on his side. He was brave enough to act and had the courage to deal with a threat that others were not prepared to face. He shows us the courage of a small person taking on a seemingly huge obstacle and winning.

☺ Questions and activities

- Draw an image to show the idea of courage.
- Write a story or a poem to show the idea of building bridges between people.
- Create a collage from magazines to celebrate the different types of people in the world. Use an A3 piece of paper. You could title it 'The Rainbow People of God', the title of a book by Archbishop Desmond Tutu of South Africa, to show that we are all valuable to God. The collage will explore the idea of having courage to let people be who they are.
- Complete the activities on the 'Courage' wisdom sheet (see page 66).

Ideas for assembly themes

- What does it mean to show courage?
- Having the courage to speak about something wrong
- Daring to be different
- Overcoming divisions between people

Wisdom sheet: Courage

Look at these ideas on courage. Choose one or more and comment on what the person is saying.

We must build dams of courage to hold back the flood of fear.
MARTIN LUTHER KING, JR

To a brave heart, nothing is impossible.
FRENCH PROVERB

Courage is what it takes to stand up and speak; courage is also what it takes to sit down and listen.
WINSTON CHURCHILL

Success is not final, failure is not fatal: it is the courage to continue that counts.
WINSTON CHURCHILL

All our dreams can come true, if we have the courage to pursue them.
WALT DISNEY

Mistakes are always forgivable, if one has the courage to admit them.
BRUCE LEE

Finish your thoughts by completing these sentences:

* I think that courage is...
* I think that I am a cowardly/courageous person because...
* The most courageous thing I have done in my life is...

✣

Celebration: Praise in the Psalms

Learning objectives

- All pupils will be able to explain the idea of celebration with reference to the Psalms.
- Most pupils will be able to explain the importance of celebration in their lives.
- Some pupils will be able to explain how celebration can help people in times of difficulty.

Starter

- When was the last time that you celebrated something? Was it a birthday or an important day like Christmas or Easter? Did the celebration live up to the excitement that you thought it might bring, or did it disappoint you instead?
- Talk about this with your partner.

Introduction

Human beings often love to have a good party to celebrate something, whether it is their birthday or a big event such as a wedding anniversary or the birth of a child. Celebrations are ways of coming together in order to focus on a significant time and perhaps to say 'thank you' to important people in our lives.

People like to think about the key moments in their lives and have a party. What we celebrate reveals what is important to us. When religious people celebrate the good things they think God has done for them, they call it 'worship', as they are trying to show how worthy God is to receive praise.

Another important reason for worship celebrations is to say 'thank you' for all the good things in life. Norman Vincent Peale wrote a book called *The Power of Positive Thinking*. In it, he showed that people who were thankful were much happier than those who moaned about everything. It is not always easy to celebrate, though, especially when we are going through a difficult time.

Look at this hymn of praise to God, celebrating his goodness to his people. Psalm 150 was written to be sung in the temple, the main place of worship in ancient Israel. Versions of this psalm are still sung or said in churches today.

Shout praises to the Lord! Praise God in his temple.
Praise him in heaven, his mighty fortress.
Praise our God!
His deeds are wonderful, too marvellous to describe.

Praise God with trumpets and all kinds of harps.
Praise him with tambourines and dancing,
with stringed instruments and woodwinds.
Praise God with cymbals, with clashing cymbals.
Let every living creature praise the Lord.
Shout praises to the Lord!
PSALM 150

Reflection

Notice how the psalm (one of the hymns in the Old Testament part of the Bible) talks about the different ways of worshipping God. We can praise God using all the different types of instruments— from trumpets to harps to cymbals. People today might praise their God in dancing, in drama, in reading the Bible, in being silent, in singing loud songs, in playing the organ or singing in the choir, in lighting candles or staying silent. There are many different ways to praise God, and each one might help people to understand or reflect on an aspect of the God they believe in.

This hymn has been sung for over 400 years as a way of giving thanks to God:

Now thank we all our God with heart and hands and voices,
Who wondrous things has done, in whom this world rejoices;
Who from our mothers' arms has blessed us on our way
With countless gifts of love, and still is ours today.

O may this bounteous God through all our life be near us,
With ever joyful hearts and blessed peace to cheer us;
And keep us in his grace and guide us when perplexed;
And free us from all ills in this world and the next!
MARTIN RINKART

☺ Questions and activities

- Write a list of the things or people that you are thankful for in your life.
- Imagine that you have been put in charge of celebrating the arrival of a new baby. What sort of things could you do to greet a new child?
- Working with a group, make a wall display to show in pictures and writing all the different ways that people celebrate God in church.
- 'We need celebrations.' What do you think? Give reasons for your answer, showing that you have thought about it from more than one point of view.
- Write a hymn of thankfulness, in which you say 'thank you' for all the good things in life.
- Plan a party for someone who has helped to support other people.
- Complete the activities on the 'Celebration' wisdom sheet (see page 71).

Ideas for assembly themes

- Celebrations
- Encouragement

Wisdom sheet: Celebration

Look at these ideas on celebration. Choose one or more and comment on what the person is saying.

Everything is created from moment to moment, always new. Like fireworks, this universe is a celebration and you are the spectator contemplating the eternal Fourth of July of your absolute splendour.
FRANCIS LUCILLE

Share our similarities, celebrate our differences.
M. SCOTT PECK

Stop worrying about the pot-holes in the road and celebrate the journey!
BARBARA HOFFMAN

The more you praise and celebrate your life, the more there is in life to celebrate.
OPRAH WINFREY

When you jump for joy, beware that no one moves the ground from beneath your feet.
STAINSLAW J. LEC

Celebrate the happiness that friends are always giving; make every day a holiday and celebrate just living!
AMANDA BARRY

Finish your thoughts by completing these sentences:

- I think that celebration is...
- Celebrations are good/bad because...
- I find it most difficult to celebrate when...

Reproduced with permission from *Emotionally Intelligent RE* by Cavan Wood (Barnabas in Schools, 2014)

+

Grief: Job's suffering

Learning objectives

- All pupils will be able to explain the idea of grief.
- Most pupils will be able to refer in detail to the story of Job.
- Some pupils will be able to reflect on their own experience of grief.

Starter

- How do you feel when you lose something? List some of the emotions that you feel.
- How do you feel when you have found a lost item again?
- Share your experiences with a partner.

Introduction

Losing someone we love is a difficult thing to face. When someone dies or moves away, we might feel an emptiness that is known as grief. We may go through many stages in order to cope with these problems. A thinker called Elizabeth Kübler Ross has suggested that there are seven stages in dealing with loss:

1. Shock and denial: for the first few weeks or months after a death or a loss, the person may deny what has happened to them, as they have been shocked.
2. Pain and guilt: a person at this stage might feel pain and guilt about not having done everything they could to help the lost one.

3. Anger and bargaining: a person might feel anger at the loss of someone. They might also decide to make a promise to themselves to live a better life, as if this will bring a person back.
4. Loneliness and depression: both of these emotions might follow.
5. Upward turn: the person who has lost another finds that they are beginning to deal with life again.
6. Working it through: the person is able to begin to run their day-to-day life.
7. Acceptance and hope: the person accepts the loss and sees hope for the future.

These stages of grief could affect someone facing not just a death but also a family break-up, moving to a new place, the end of a friendship or any other changes that might happen to us suddenly.

In the story of Job in the Bible, a very rich man with a large and loving family suddenly has everything he loves and values taken away from him. In the book named after him, we see how Job copes with the suffering he faces. A group of people turn up and try to tell him why the bad things have happened to him. They are sometimes called 'Job's comforters', which is a bit sarcastic, as they often say some very harsh and unfair things to him.

This passage shows Job at the lowest point of grief.

Why does God let me live
when life is miserable and so bitter?
I keep longing for death
more than I would seek a valuable treasure.
Nothing could make me happier than to be in the grave.
Why do I go on living when God has me surrounded,
and I can't see the road?
Moaning and groaning are my food and drink,
and my worst fears have all come true.
I have no peace or rest—
only troubles and worries.

JOB 3:20–26

Reflection

This is one of Job's responses to what has happened to him. He listens to the 'comforters', all of whom seem to think that he must have done something bad to make all the bad things happen to him. He says that he has not. Towards the end of the book, there is a storm and, in the middle of the storm, God speaks to Job. God tells Job that he will never be able to understand why some things happen. God alone knows why they happen, not any human being.

Looking at the power of God in the storm, Job realises how small he is in comparison with God. At the end of the book, all the things that he has lost are restored to him, with more besides: he has come through the grief as a stronger person, trusting less in himself and more in God. He has also realised that bad things happen to people who may not have done anything particularly wrong to cause them. Some things just happen. What matters is how we react to them.

☺ Questions and activities

- How can we help each other in times when we are grieving the loss of someone?
- Design a card for someone who has lost someone, or write a poem to help them deal with their sense of loss.
- Write a list of things that you should not say when someone is upset.
- Create a classroom display of big, difficult questions about life.
- Complete the activities on the 'Grief' wisdom sheet (see page 76).

Ideas for assembly themes

- Grief and bereavement
- Dealing with difficult times

Wisdom sheet: Grief

Look at these ideas on grief. Choose one or more and comment on what the person is saying.

No one ever told me that grief felt so like fear.
C.S. LEWIS

To weep is to make less the depth of grief.
WILLIAM SHAKESPEARE

Grief is a most peculiar thing; we're so helpless in the face of it. It's like a window that will simply open of its own accord. The room grows cold, and we can do nothing but shiver. But it opens a little less each time and a little less; and one day we wonder what has become of it.
ARTHUR GOLDEN

Time is a physician that heals every grief.
DIPHILUS

No one ever really dies as long as they took the time to leave us with fond memories.
CHRIS SORENSEN

Finish your thoughts by completing these sentences:

- I think that grief is...
- Grieving is good/bad because...
- I find it most difficult to grieve when...
- I was most upset when...

Reproduced with permission from *Emotionally Intelligent RE* by Cavan Wood (Barnabas in Schools, 2014)

✢

Wisdom and knowledge:
The book of Proverbs

Learning objectives

- All pupils will be able to explain the ideas of wisdom and knowledge.
- Most pupils will be able to give details of these ideas with reference to the biblical understanding of them.
- Some pupils will be able to make comments on their own ideas of wisdom.

Starter

Look at these sayings:

- Many hands make light work.
- Too many cooks spoil the broth.

What do you think they mean? Can both be true?

Introduction

What is wisdom and what is knowledge? Someone once said that knowledge is knowing that a tomato is a fruit, but wisdom is not putting it in a fruit salad. In the Bible, wisdom is about showing a common-sense approach to the world, and showing love and respect to others. Knowledge is simply the gathering of facts, which does not necessarily help other people.

A person once described their older friend as wise. The friend pointed out that what the younger person called 'wisdom' was due merely to the fact that the older person had had more time to make mistakes and learn from them; wisdom was not a gift they had been given or a natural talent.

Life will involve making mistakes; what we have to do is to see if we can learn from them, move on and try to learn ways not to make the same mistakes again. Wisdom is not just in the head, but it is about how we live with and behave towards other people.

Let's look at a passage in the Bible that talks about wisdom.

Honest correction is appreciated more than flattery.
If you cheat your parents and don't think it's wrong,
you are a common thief.
Selfish people cause trouble,
but you will live a full life if you trust the Lord.
Only fools would trust what they alone think,
but if you live by wisdom, you will do all right.

Giving to the poor will keep you from poverty,
but if you close your eyes to their needs,
everyone will curse you.
When crooks are in control, everyone tries to hide,
but when they lose power, good people are everywhere.
PROVERBS 28:23–28

Reflection

In the book of Proverbs, there are different ways of looking at the idea of wisdom. For the writers, wisdom is often linked with trusting in the Lord, making sure that God is at the centre of life. It is also important to realise that wisdom isn't just about how we think but about how we live. When we avoid stealing and we give to others in need, that is wise behaviour—and not just because we are following the rules or thinking that if we help someone today they will be in our debt.

A wise person may not be intelligent in the sense of being good at tests or having lots of exam certificates. They may not know a great deal about many subjects, but they do know this: a wise life is one where we make other lives better and use the time we have as well as we can. Foolishness is when we don't care about ourselves or others.

☺ Questions and activities

- What is the difference between wisdom and foolishness? You could explain it by drawing two columns marked 'Wisdom' and 'Foolishness' and listing appropriate descriptions under each heading.
- Give examples of a foolish piece of behaviour and a wise piece of behaviour. Why did you choose these examples? Give reasons for the choices that you have made.
- Draw an image to show the ideas of wisdom and foolishness.
- Read the following story from Aesop's *Fables*. What might it teach us about wisdom and foolishness?

A Hare one day ridiculed the short feet and slow pace of the Tortoise, who replied, laughing, 'Though you be swift as the wind, I will beat you in a race.' The Hare, believing her assertion to be simply impossible, assented to the proposal; and they agreed that the Fox should choose the course and fix the goal.

On the day appointed for the race, the two started together. The Tortoise never for a moment stopped, but went on with a slow but steady pace straight to the end of the course. The Hare, lying down by the wayside, fell fast asleep. At last waking up, and moving as fast as he could, he saw the Tortoise had reached the goal, and was comfortably dozing after her fatigue.

Moral: slow but steady wins the race.

- Complete the activities on the 'Wisdom and knowledge' wisdom sheet (see page 81).

Ideas for assembly themes

- The difference between wisdom and knowledge
- Wise behaviour
- The tortoise and the hare—slow but steady

Wisdom sheet: Wisdom and knowledge

Look at these ideas on wisdom and knowledge. Choose one or more and comment on what the person is saying.

A good head and a good heart are always a formidable combination.
NELSON MANDELA

A wise man is superior to any insults which can be put upon him, and the best reply to unseemly behaviour is patience and moderation.
MOLIÈRE

There is wisdom of the head, and wisdom of the heart.
CHARLES DICKENS

Good nature is worth more than knowledge, more than money, more than honour, to the persons who possess it.
HENRY WARD BEECHER

Wisdom begins in wonder.
SOCRATES

Turn your wounds into wisdom.
OPRAH WINFREY

Wise men change their lives; fools seldom do.
ENGLISH PROVERB

Finish your thoughts by completing these sentences:

- I think that wisdom is...
- I think foolishness is...
- On balance, I think I am a wise/foolish person because...

Reproduced with permission from *Emotionally Intelligent RE* by Cavan Wood (Barnabas in Schools, 2014)

✢

Despair: Ecclesiastes

Learning objectives

- All pupils will be able to explain the idea of despair.
- Most pupils will be able to show the reasons why people might feel like this, and to use some biblical teaching to show their understanding of it.
- Some pupils will be able to comment on how the teaching of Ecclesiastes might help stop feelings of despair from developing.

Starter

- Draw or write about three things that, if they happened to you today, might make it a bad day.

Introduction

We all have bad days. Here is a story about one.

Dave had had a bad day at school. His teacher had snapped at him when he had not done as he was told. He'd had a fight with someone he thought was a friend, and everyone had seemed to be taking the other boy's side. Then, when he got home, his mum had had a go at him about the state of his bedroom and how he needed to clear it up. At supper time, he'd had to eat the terrible food that his mum put in front of him, and his dad had told him off when he was rude to his mum about her cooking. As he lay in bed that night, Dave thought to himself, 'What is the point?'

Three thousand years ago, there was a king called Solomon. Many people believe that he wrote a book called Ecclesiastes as a way of expressing his feelings that his life was empty and pointless. He had wealth, power and a family life, but he was not a happy person. Something was missing, and that was happiness with the life he was leading. He began to write down his thoughts to help him think through what was important in life and what was not.

Nothing makes sense! Everything is nonsense.
I have seen it all—nothing makes sense!
What is there to show for all of our hard work
here on this earth?
People come, and people go,
but still the world never changes.

The sun comes up, the sun goes down;
it hurries right back to where it started from.
The wind blows south, the wind blows north;
round and round it blows over and over again.
All rivers empty into the sea, but it never spills over;
one by one the rivers return to their source.

All of life is far more boring than words could ever say.
Our eyes and our ears are never satisfied
with what we see and hear.
Everything that happens has happened before;
nothing is new, nothing under the sun.
Someone might say, 'Here is something new!'
But it happened before, long before we were born.
ECCLESIASTES 1:2–10

Reflection

The emptiness that the king felt all those years ago can still affect people today, and, in those desperate moments, there is a need to make sure that people can be helped.

Beachy Head is a famous cliff in Sussex where many people over the years have committed suicide by jumping off. A few years ago, a group from the local churches met up with the police and emergency services and suggested asking volunteers to stand near the cliff: if the volunteers saw people approaching who seemed likely to be intending to jump, they would talk to them and encourage them to think again about whether it was the right thing to do.

As a result, the Beachy Head Chaplaincy Team was set up as a charity, saving the lives of suicidal people at Beachy Head. They are a Christian chaplaincy, specialising in crisis intervention and search and rescue. The team is made up largely of volunteers, who are all Christians and active members of local church congregations. To give one example, they were involved in 21 incidents and searches during the week ending 26 August 2012, resulting in the rescue of seven people who might have committed suicide had they not intervened. As a consequence of the charity's work, many people have decided not to take their own lives after all but have asked for help and have begun to sort out the problems they faced.

☺ Questions and activities

- Many things can make us sad or unhappy. One way to deal with these feelings is to think positively. Try listing all the things that you could be grateful about.
- Draw an image to show the idea of despair.
- Read chapter 1 of the book of Job in the Bible. How does Job deal with his problems?

- Write a job description for a person wanting to be a member of the chaplaincy team at Beachy Head.
- Complete the activities on the 'Despair' wisdom sheet (see page 86).

Ideas for assembly themes

- Dealing with the times when we feel low
- Being a good listener when people need our help

Wisdom sheet: Despair

Look at these ideas on despair. Choose one or more and comment on what the person is saying.

Despair gives courage to a coward.
THOMAS FULLER

Despair has its own calms.
BRAM STOKER

Despair is a narcotic. It lulls the mind into indifference.
CHARLIE CHAPLIN

I have plumbed the depths of despair and have found them not bottomless.
THOMAS HARDY

Despair is the conclusion of fools.
BENJAMIN DISRAELI

Despair is the damp of hell, as joy is the serenity of heaven.
JOHN DONNE

I do believe that most men live lives of quiet desperation. For despair, optimism is the only practical solution. Hope is practical. Because eliminate that and it's pretty scary. Hope at least gives you the option of living.
HARRY NILSSON

Finish your thoughts by completing these sentences:

* I think that despair is…
* On the whole, I have a positive/negative outlook on life because…

Reproduced with permission from *Emotionally Intelligent RE* by Cavan Wood (Barnabas in Schools, 2014)

✛

Hope: The prophet Isaiah

Learning objectives

- All pupils will be able to explain the idea of hope as shown by Isaiah.
- Some pupils will be able to give detailed examples of how hope can help people now.
- Most pupils will be able to comment on why some people find it difficult to have a hopeful approach to the future.

Starter

- What things make you excited and hopeful?

Introduction

In the Greek story of Pandora's box, Pandora is given a box within which all bad things are kept. She is told not to open it, but her curiosity gets the better of her. When she opens the box, all the bad things come out into the world. However, there is one thing still left at the bottom of the box—the quality of hope. The world might be a difficult and evil place at times, but this story shows that, with the spirit of hope, we can see change.

Jürgen Moltmann went though World War II as a German soldier and prisoner of war. When he returned to Germany, he discovered the full horror of what had happened in the Holocaust as well as seeing how his homeland had been battered. He decided that his country needed what he called 'a theology of hope': people needed to realise that hope was a gift from God that would enable them to make a better world.

In the 1980s, South Africa was a very racist country. Eddy Grant had a hit with a song called 'Give me hope, Joanna', Joanna being a nickname for the country's capital city Johannesburg. That hope was realised when, in 1994, South Africa ended its way of running that country, which was called 'apartheid', a form of racism that picked on black people.

The biblical prophet Isaiah, too, spoke to a people who did not have much hope for the future. In Isaiah's day, Israel had been invaded and many of its people had been taken away to another country. He gave them the following promise from God:

Our God has said:
'Encourage my people!
Give them comfort.
Speak kindly to Jerusalem
and announce:
Your slavery is past;
your punishment is over.
I, the Lord, made you pay
double for your sins.'

Someone is shouting:
'Clear a path in the desert!
Make a straight road
for the Lord our God.
Fill in the valleys;
flatten every hill
and mountain.
Level the rough
and rugged ground.
Then the glory of the Lord
will appear for all to see.
The Lord has promised this.'
ISAIAH 40:1–5

Reflection

Some of these words from Isaiah were used by Martin Luther King in his famous speech 'I have a dream', as a way to encourage people to pursue justice for all Americans, both black and white. He knew that these words had the power to make people hopeful, and that when people had hope they could be brave.

Hope is a good thing if it leads to the belief that changes can happen and it is possible to make a better world. The singer Sam Cooke had a song called 'A change is gonna come'. This was his way of saying that no matter how bad it felt, being on the receiving end of racism, there would be an end to the problems.

In the Democratic Republic of Congo, there are many children living on the streets. They become homeless for a number of reasons, including their parents' deaths from AIDS or malaria. Some people in the UK and France decided to act, and built a house to home many of the children. This enabled a charity to develop, called Kimbilio, which could help to feed, educate and support some very damaged children. Many people had given up on the children, but this project was an act of hope, showing them that they mattered.

Once we act, either by ourselves or with others, then we can bring hope and make the world a better place.

☺ Questions and activities

- What are your hopes in life? What would you like to achieve?
- Prophecy is about giving hope for the future and saying what is wrong about the present. Draw some things that you would like to happen in the future. They might be inventions or an end to world problems such as starvation or war.
- Write a speech about the hopes that you have for the world, your school or your family.

- Design a board game that encourages people to think about the things that give them hope.
- Complete the activities on the 'Hope' wisdom sheet (see page 91).

Ideas for assembly themes

- Having a positive outlook
- Planning for the future

Wisdom sheet: Hope

Look at these ideas on hope. Choose one or more and comment on what the person is saying.

Hope springs eternal in the human breast;
Man never is, but always to be blest.
ALEXANDER POPE

We have always held to the hope, the belief, the conviction that there is a better life, a better world, beyond the horizon.
FRANKLIN D. ROOSEVELT

While there's life, there's hope.
MARCUS TULLIUS CICERO

The youth is the hope of our future.
JOSE RIZAL

Everything that is done in the world is done by hope.
MARTIN LUTHER KING, JR

I hope that I may always desire more than I can accomplish.
MICHELANGELO

Those who hope for no other life are dead even for this.
JOHANN WOLFGANG VON GOETHE

Finish your thoughts by completing these sentences:

- I think that hope is...
- I think that without hope...
- The greatest hope I have for this school is that...
- The greatest hope I have for my own life is that...

Reproduced with permission from *Emotionally Intelligent RE* by Cavan Wood (Barnabas in Schools, 2014)

✣

Moaning and complaining: Jonah

Learning objectives

- All pupils will be able to explain what moaning is and to see why it is a negative habit.
- Most pupils will be able to comment on Jonah's moaning.
- Some pupils will be able to think of alternatives to moaning.

Starter

- What sort of things make you upset about life?
- Are you right to get upset about these things?

Introduction

There are some things wrong in the world that we can and should get upset about. When people are not treated fairly, it is right to want their treatment to change. Sometimes, though, we moan: we complain when we are bored or when we don't want to do something that will be difficult for us to do. We might see people on the television or hear them on the radio moaning. Some people love to complain, but does this really help them to cope with the way that the world is? Does it help to make the world better? No, it does not.

According to surveys, people who have a more positive outlook on life tend to live longer and have better mental and physical health.

The biblical prophet Jonah is an example of someone who moaned. He did not like the fact that God had asked him to go and tell the people of the city of Nineveh to repent, to turn back from the evil that they were doing. He tried to sail away to a city in the opposite direction, but a great storm blew up. Jonah was thrown overboard by the worried sailors, and, according to the story, was swallowed by a big fish. After a few days, he found himself on the beach just outside the city of Nineveh. Very reluctantly, he shared God's message with the people there. Then, instead of being happy when they changed their ways, he began to moan and complain about how merciful and loving God was, so God decided to teach him a lesson.

Jonah was really upset and angry. So he prayed:

'Our Lord, I knew from the very beginning that you wouldn't destroy Nineveh. That's why I left my own country and headed for Spain. You are a kind and merciful God, and you are very patient. You always show love, and you don't like to punish anyone, not even foreigners. Now let me die! I'd be better off dead.'

The Lord replied, 'What right do you have to be angry?'

Jonah then left through the east gate of the city and made a shelter to protect himself from the sun. He sat under the shelter, waiting to see what would happen to Nineveh.

The Lord made a vine grow up to shade Jonah's head and protect him from the sun. Jonah was very happy to have the vine, but early the next morning the Lord sent a worm to chew on the vine, and the vine dried up. During the day the Lord sent a scorching wind, and the sun beat down on Jonah's head, making him feel faint. Jonah was ready to die, and he shouted, 'I wish I were dead!'

But the Lord asked, 'Jonah, do you have the right to be angry about the vine?'

'Yes, I do,' he answered, 'and I'm angry enough to die.'

But the Lord said: 'You are concerned about a vine that you did not plant or take care of, a vine that grew up in one night and died the next. In that city of Nineveh there are more than a hundred and twenty thousand people who cannot tell right from

wrong, and many cattle are also there. Don't you think I should be concerned about that big city?'
JONAH 4:1–11

Reflection

Jonah's behaviour over the tree that sprang up in a day and then died is a little odd, to say the least. He had not understood how much God loved everyone—including the people in Nineveh, whom he had written off. He was wrong to get upset and complain about something that, according to the story, saved a city from destruction.

☺ Questions and activities

- Why was Jonah told by God to go to Nineveh?
- Why did Jonah not want to go?
- When they heard Jonah's message, the people of Nineveh were able to say 'sorry' to God. How easy do you find it to say 'sorry' when you are wrong?
- Should doing a good thing always make you feel good? Give reasons for your answer, showing that you have thought about it from more than one point of view.
- 'People should complain less and try to do more to make the world a better place.' What do you think? Give reasons for your answer, showing that you have thought about it from more than one point of view.
- Complete the activities on the 'Moaning and complaining' wisdom sheet (see page 96).

Ideas for assembly themes

- Seeing the good in bad situations
- Trying to be positive

Wisdom sheet: Moaning and complaining

Look at these ideas on moaning and complaining. Choose one or more and comment on what the person is saying.

Everyone has to make their own decisions. I still believe in that. You just have to be able to accept the consequences without complaining.
GRACE JONES

When you're in a situation, you can complain about it, you can feel sorry for yourself, you can do a lot of things. But how are you gonna make the situation better?
TONY DUNGY

Man invented language to satisfy his deep need to complain.
LILY TOMLIN

Any fool can criticise, condemn and complain—and most fools do.
BENJAMIN FRANKLIN

The future rewards those who press on. I don't have time to feel sorry for myself. I don't have time to complain. I'm going to press on.
BARACK OBAMA

Finish your thoughts by completing these sentences:

- I think that moaning is...
- I think that without moaning...
- In order to stop myself moaning I will...

Reproduced with permission from *Emotionally Intelligent RE* by Cavan Wood (Barnabas in Schools, 2014)

+

Acceptance: The woman who washed Jesus' feet

Learning objectives

- All pupils will be able to explain the idea of acceptance, with reference to the story of the woman anointing Jesus.
- Most pupils will be able to show the idea of acceptance in action.
- Some pupils will be able to explain whether some people should not be accepted.

Starter

- What do you find difficult to accept in other people?
- How do you deal with these emotions?

Introduction

According to some experts, we can decide what we think about someone we are meeting for the first time within a few seconds of looking at the other person's face. This can, however, mean that we make mistakes about what the person is really like. For example, the person might be quiet and we assume that they are being rude, but it might be that they are quite shy when meeting new people.

Sometimes, we find it hard to accept others because we have been encouraged to judge people for being different from us. We can say or do things that really hurt other people and not realise just how badly we have behaved by doing so. We might have been influenced to think in judgemental ways by our family or friends, or we might have had a bad experience with a particular type of person, or perhaps we do not really understand what it is like to be someone else.

Many religions teach that we should treat other people as we would like to be treated ourselves. We know this as the 'Golden Rule'. In the story below, Jesus encounters a person who has not been accepted by others.

A Pharisee invited Jesus to have dinner with him. So Jesus went to the Pharisee's home and got ready to eat.

When a sinful woman in that town found out that Jesus was there, she bought an expensive bottle of perfume. Then she came and stood behind Jesus. She cried and started washing his feet with her tears and drying them with her hair. The woman kissed his feet and poured the perfume on them.

The Pharisee who had invited Jesus saw this and said to himself, 'If this man really were a prophet, he would know what kind of woman is touching him! He would know that she is a sinner.'

Jesus said to the Pharisee, 'Simon, I have something to say to you.'

'Teacher, what is it?' Simon replied.

Jesus told him, 'Two people were in debt to a moneylender. One of them owed him five hundred silver coins, and the other owed him fifty. Since neither of them could pay him back, the moneylender said that they didn't have to pay him anything. Which one of them will like him more?'

Simon answered, 'I suppose it would be the one who had owed more and didn't have to pay it back.'

'You are right,' Jesus said.

He turned towards the woman and said to Simon, 'Have you noticed this woman? When I came into your home, you didn't give me any water so I could wash my feet. But she has washed my feet with her tears and dried them with her hair. You didn't greet me with a kiss, but from the time I came in, she has not stopped kissing my feet. You didn't even pour olive oil on my head, but she has poured expensive perfume on my feet. So I tell you that all her sins are forgiven, and that is why she has shown great love. But anyone who has been forgiven for only a little will show only a little love.'

Then Jesus said to the woman, 'Your sins are forgiven.'

Some other guests started saying to one another, 'Who is this who dares to forgive sins?'

But Jesus told the woman, 'Because of your faith, you are now saved. May God give you peace!'

LUKE 7:36–50

Reflection

Here was a woman who was desperate to be accepted, to be understood, to be encouraged. When she poured out the perfume on Jesus' feet, she was taking a risk, as he would not necessarily have reacted with acceptance. As a holy teacher, he could have rejected her. Yet that is not Jesus' way. He shows in a number of his encounters, and in the stories he tells, that he values all people, regardless of their history.

The Langley House Trust was set up by a group of Christian businesspeople who wished to show their faith in practice by helping ex-prisoners readjust to the outside world. Nationally, 70 out of every 100 ex-prisoners return to jail. Among the people whom Langley House has worked with, that figure is two out of every 100. These Christian businesspeople believe that whatever a person has done, they should be accepted.

☺ Questions and activities

- A famous song has the title 'I am what I am'. What does this mean? Does it mean we should not try to change ourselves for the better?
- Design a poster about the reasons why we should take time before judging other people.
- Which types of punishment are acceptable and which are not? Give reasons for your answers.
- Write a list of crimes and what you think their punishments should be.
- Complete the activities on the 'Acceptance' wisdom sheet (see page 101).

Ideas for assembly themes

- Accepting differences
- Not judging

Wisdom sheet: Acceptance

Look at these ideas on acceptance. Choose one or more and comment on what the person is saying.

Acceptance and tolerance and forgiveness, those are life-altering lessons.
JESSICA LANGE

The art of acceptance is the art of making someone who has just done you a small favour wish that he might have done you a greater one.
MARTIN LUTHER KING, JR

The first step toward change is awareness. The second step is acceptance.
NATHANIEL BRANDEN

At the heart of personality is the need to feel a sense of being lovable without having to qualify for that acceptance.
PAUL TOURNIER

The acceptance of death gives you more of a stake in life, in living life happily, as it should be lived—living for the moment.
STING

Finish your thoughts by completing these sentences:

- I feel that acceptance of others means that...
- I have sometimes not felt accepted when...
- One of the ways to encourage people to be more accepting is to...

Reproduced with permission from *Emotionally Intelligent RE* by Cavan Wood (Barnabas in Schools, 2014)

＋

Being selfish: Zacchaeus

Learning objectives

- All pupils will be able to explain what selfishness is and why people behave selfishly.
- Most pupils will be able to offer some solutions to this problem.
- Some pupils will be able to assess the pros and cons of selfishness.

Starter

- Why do you think that people are selfish? How could you encourage people to move away from being selfish?
- Discuss this with a partner and write down your ideas.

Introduction

The scientist Richard Dawkins has suggested that our genes are selfish: they make sure that they survive, whatever the cost. Some people think that when Charles Darwin talked about 'the survival of the fittest', he meant that you had to have a certain amount of selfishness to go on living. (Darwin actually meant that an animal was more likely to survive if it was best adapted to its environment, not necessarily if it was more aggressive.)

Other people would say that we learn to be selfish, not because our genes programme us to be so, but because we realise that this is the only way in which we can survive and get our way. We might also learn, however, that certain ways of behaving make people like us more, which quite often can involve being less selfish. Even then, a person might behave less selfishly in one way so that they can be more loved and feel better about who they are—an emotion that could fundamentally be quite selfish.

Are we preprogrammed or free to make our choices, including the choice to be selfish? Christians see selfishness as one of the worst sins—something that breaks down the relationship that God wants to have with human beings.

Do we control this urge or does it control us? Let us look at a man in the Bible who moved from being selfish to selfless and consider how he came to the point of change. Notice Jesus' reaction to this man. Is it what you would expect?

Jesus was going through Jericho, where a man named Zacchaeus lived. He was in charge of collecting taxes and was very rich. Jesus was heading his way, and Zacchaeus wanted to see what he was like. But Zacchaeus was a short man and could not see over the crowd. So he ran ahead and climbed up into a sycamore tree.

When Jesus got there, he looked up and said, 'Zacchaeus, hurry down! I want to stay with you today.' Zacchaeus hurried down and gladly welcomed Jesus.

Everyone who saw this started grumbling, 'This man Zacchaeus is a sinner! And Jesus is going home to eat with him.'

Later that day Zacchaeus stood up and said to the Lord, 'I will give half of my property to the poor. And I will now pay back four times as much to everyone I have ever cheated.'

Jesus said to Zacchaeus, 'Today you and your family have been saved, because you are a true son of Abraham. The Son of Man came to look for and to save people who are lost.'

LUKE 19:1–10

Reflection

The consequences of selfishness are staggering. In 2013, there are roughly seven billion people on the planet, but 2.6 billion of them—four out of every ten people alive—do not have a safe, private or clean place to go to the toilet. Two groups, Cord and Tearfund, decided to do something about this and came up with the idea of twinning toilets: a person in the UK can pay for a place in a poorer country to have a toilet that is safe, private and clean (and gets a certificate to hang in their own bathroom). In the first three years of their work, Cord and Tearfund have been able to build 1600 toilets for over 10,000 people in the African country of Burundi.

In his book *Affluenza*, Oliver James said that one of the problems for many people in countries like the UK and the USA is that they are unhappy because they spend a lot of time trying to get more money and power. They think their money will buy them happiness but it actually makes them more miserable. What makes people happy, Oliver James believes, is belonging to families and communities that make them feel valued, not pursuing a selfish lifestyle. In other words, if we want to be happy, we cannot be alone with our money, as Zacchaeus was at the beginning of the story. When Jesus invited himself to go and eat at his house, he was showing he accepted Zacchaeus.

☺ Questions and activities

- How might you have expected Jesus to treat Zacchaeus? Why do you think Jesus treated him in the way that he did?
- What would be the most difficult of your possessions to give up, and why?
- 'We must live more simply so that others may simply live.' What does this sentence mean?
- Devise a game in which the players have to cooperate with each other to win.
- Complete the activities on the 'Being selfish' wisdom sheet (see page 106).

Ideas for assembly themes

- Being selfish
- Jesus' teaching on money
- Generosity
- Working with others

Wisdom sheet: Being selfish

Look at these ideas on selfishness. Choose one or more and comment on what the person is saying.

Selfishness is that detestable vice which no one will forgive in others, and no one is without himself.
HENRY WARD BEECHER

Selfishness is the greatest curse of the human race.
WILLIAM E. GLADSTONE

Selfishness must always be forgiven, you know, because there is no hope of a cure.
JANE AUSTEN

Nine-tenths of our unhappiness is selfishness and is an insult cast in the face of God.
G.H. MORRISON

When a man is wrapped up in himself, he makes a pretty small package.
JOHN RUSKIN

Finish your thoughts by completing these sentences:

• I think that selfishness is…
• I think that I am a selfless/selfish person because…

Reproduced with permission from *Emotionally Intelligent RE* by Cavan Wood (Barnabas in Schools, 2014)

✛

Denial and lying: Peter

Learning objectives

- All pupils will be able to explain the idea of denial, with reference to the story of Peter.
- Most pupils will be able to refer to their own experience of denial.
- Some pupils will be able to consider other reasons why denial happens.

Starter

- When do you find it hard to say what you believe?
- Have you ever let anyone down by saying one thing and doing another?

Introduction

What do you do in a situation where you are put under pressure by other people? It is easy sometimes to give in. Peer pressure happens when one or more of your 'peers' (people in your own group of friends, perhaps) puts pressure on you to behave or believe differently from the way you would if you were making your own choices. Sometimes, peer pressure can be good—perhaps persuading someone to stop being racist; sometimes it might not be so good, encouraging a person to do something wrong, like stealing. We all have the experience at times of trying to pretend we are something we are not.

One of Jesus' disciples, Peter, made a promise that he would never let Jesus down. It was broken just a few hours after Jesus was arrested, when Peter pretended not to know him as he became afraid for his own safety.

Jesus was arrested and led away to the house of the high priest, while Peter followed at a distance. Some people built a fire in the middle of the courtyard and were sitting around it. Peter sat there with them, and a servant girl saw him. Then after she had looked at him carefully, she said, 'This man was with Jesus!'

Peter said, 'Woman, I don't even know that man!'

A little later someone else saw Peter and said, 'You are one of them!'

'No, I'm not!' Peter replied.

About an hour later another man insisted, 'This man must have been with Jesus. They both come from Galilee.'

Peter replied, 'I don't know what you are talking about!' At once, while Peter was still speaking, a cock crowed.

The Lord turned and looked at Peter. And Peter remembered that the Lord had said, 'Before a cock crows tomorrow morning, you will say three times that you don't know me.' Then Peter went out and cried hard.

LUKE 22:54–62

Reflection

Could there be anything worse than feeling that someone has let you down—unless it is knowing that you have let someone else down? Peter denied, three times, that he even knew Jesus. Notice how Jesus deals with this in the next passage, which takes place after Jesus has come back to life.

When Jesus and his disciples had finished eating, he asked, 'Simon son of John, do you love me more than the others do?'

Simon Peter answered, 'Yes, Lord, you know I do!'

'Then feed my lambs,' Jesus said.

Jesus asked a second time, 'Simon son of John, do you love me?'

Peter answered, 'Yes, Lord, you know I love you!'

'Then take care of my sheep,' Jesus told him.

Jesus asked a third time, 'Simon son of John, do you love me?'

Peter was hurt because Jesus had asked him three times if he loved him. So he told Jesus, 'Lord, you know everything. You know I love you.'

Jesus replied, 'Feed my sheep. I tell you for certain that when you were a young man, you dressed yourself and went wherever you wanted to go. But when you are old, you will hold out your hands. Then others will tie your belt around you and lead you where you don't want to go.'

Jesus said this to tell how Peter would die and bring honour to God. Then he said to Peter, 'Follow me!'

JOHN 21:15–19

Could you be as forgiving as Jesus is here? He takes Peter through the memory of denying him three times, by asking him to affirm his love for Jesus three times. Three times a mistake was made: to be restored three times would help Peter receive healing for the regret that he felt.

☺ Questions and activities

- Write a version of the story of Peter's denial and acceptance.
- How do you deal with situations in which you know that someone has lied to you?
- Are there promises that are impossible to keep? How do you deal with the fact that people will let you down?
- Read the story of the prodigal son in Luke 15:11–30. How might recalling that story have helped Peter deal with the denial he had made?
- Complete the activities on the 'Denial and lying' wisdom sheet (see page 111).

Ideas for assembly themes

- Dealing with being disappointed by others
- Peer pressure

Wisdom sheet: Denial and lying

Look at these thoughts about lying and denial. Choose one or more and comment on what the person is saying.

To hide a fault with a lie is to replace a blot with a hole.
MARCUS AURELIUS

We lie loudest when we lie to ourselves.
ERIC HOFFER

No man has a good enough memory to make a successful liar.
ABRAHAM LINCOLN

A lie can travel halfway around the world while the truth is putting on its shoes.
MARK TWAIN

Lying can never save us from another lie.
VACLAV HAVEL

The worst lies are the lies we tell ourselves. We live in denial of what we do, even what we think. We do this because we're afraid.
RICHARD BACH

Delay is the deadliest form of denial.
C. NORTHCOTE PARKINSON

Finish your thoughts by completing these sentences:

- I think that I have/have not lied to myself...
- I think there can be/cannot be white lies because...
- People always need to face up to the truth about themselves and others because...

Reproduced with permission from *Emotionally Intelligent RE* by Cavan Wood (Barnabas in Schools, 2014)

+

Doubt: Thomas

Learning objectives

- All pupils will be able to explain the idea of doubt with reference to the story of Thomas.
- Most pupils will be able to see the story of Thomas as a way to help people of faith.
- Some pupils will be able to see the story of Thomas in both positive and negative terms.

Starter

- What does the word 'doubt' mean? Work with a partner to come up with a definition.
- Are you a doubting or a trusting person? Why do you think you are the way you are? Ask someone who knows you to comment.

Introduction

The story of Thomas has led to a phrase that we use in English. 'Doubting Thomas' is a way of describing a person who has found it difficult to believe in something that they have not seen for themselves.

What is doubt? One dictionary defines it as 'a feeling of uncertainty or lack of conviction'. But it would not be sensible to believe completely in ourselves all the time. Sometimes, doubt can keep us from being big-headed. It can also make us realise that believing in someone or some cause is not always wise.

In this story of Jesus and Thomas, we see how Thomas's doubt turned to faith.

Although Thomas the Twin was one of the twelve disciples, he wasn't with the others when Jesus appeared to them. So they told him, 'We have seen the Lord!'

But Thomas said, 'First, I must see the nail scars in his hands and touch them with my finger. I must put my hand where the spear went into his side. I won't believe unless I do this!'

A week later the disciples were together again. This time, Thomas was with them. Jesus came in while the doors were still locked and stood in the middle of the group. He greeted his disciples and said to Thomas, 'Put your finger here and look at my hands! Put your hand into my side. Stop doubting and have faith!'

Thomas replied, 'You are my Lord and my God!'

Jesus said, 'Thomas, do you have faith because you have seen me? The people who have faith in me without seeing me are the ones who are really blessed!'

JOHN 20:24–29

Reflection

Thomas thought that seeing the risen Jesus would be the way in which he could come to faith. Jesus, when he does appear, challenges him and then adds that people who believe but have not seen are even more blessed. But does seeing something mean that we can or should believe in it?

According to tradition, Thomas later travelled to India to share his Christian faith there. The doubter had become the believer. He was able to encourage people who found it difficult to believe.

There are many things that we might find difficult to believe. For some, it is the idea of the existence of God. Others find it difficult to believe that they can achieve things or that they are of value. When we doubt ourselves and our ability to do something, we need to ask people around us whether this really is the case. We can underestimate or overestimate what we are capable of achieving. We need to work towards having a correct view of ourselves.

😃 Questions and activities

- Why do you think Thomas behaved in the way that he did? How would you have reacted if you had been in the room?
- People often doubt themselves and their own abilities. We need to encourage each other. Taking a piece of paper, write down three things you really like about a person in the room. Then ask them to write the things they like about you on your sheet.
- Draw an image to show the idea of doubt.
- Why might doubt sometimes be a good thing? When might it be a bad thing? Give reasons for your answers.
- Find out about Christianity in India. Design a wall display, making sure that you have included information about Thomas and his role in bringing Christian faith to the country.
- Complete the activities on the 'Doubt' wisdom sheet (see page 115).

Ideas for assembly themes

- How to make up your mind
- Dealing with doubts
- Having a right view of ourselves
- Encouraging and affirming others

Wisdom sheet: Doubt

Look at these ideas on doubt. Choose one or more and comment on what the person is saying.

Doubt is part of all religion. All the religious thinkers were doubters.
ISAAC BASHEVIS SINGER

Doubt, of whatever kind, can be ended by action alone.
THOMAS CARLYLE

People may doubt what you say, but they will believe what you do.
LEWIS CASS

Never doubt that you can change history. You already have.
MARGE PIERCY

The wise are prone to doubt.
GREEK PROVERB

Our doubts are traitors,
And make us lose the good we oft might win
By fearing to attempt.
WILLIAM SHAKESPEARE

Doubt is the beginning, not the end of wisdom.
ENGLISH PROVERB

Finish your thoughts by completing these sentences:

- I think that doubt is…
- I doubt when…
- I find it easier to believe and not doubt when…
- I think that doubt is a good/bad thing because…

Reproduced with permission from *Emotionally Intelligent RE* by Cavan Wood (Barnabas in Schools, 2014)

+

Misunderstanding: Paul in Athens

Learning objectives

- All pupils will be able to explain what it means to be misunderstood.
- Most pupils will be able to explain how Paul was misunderstood in Athens.
- Some pupils will be able to explain how we can avoid being misunderstood.

Starter

Play a game of Chinese Whispers as a class. The teacher will give the first person a message to be whispered round the class, and then the last person has to say what message they received. How different are the two messages from each other?

Introduction

The pop group The Animals had a song called 'Please don't let me be misunderstood'. Being misunderstood is a very common experience. People can 'get the wrong end of the stick'—that is, they do not understand what the other person is saying.

There are many reasons why we might misunderstand someone:

- We might not have listened to them, and therefore don't understand why they are behaving in the way that they are.
- We might not have had the experiences the other person has had and cannot see things from their point of view.
- Someone else might have influenced us wrongly about what the person said or did.

The most common reason why we are misunderstood is that there has been a lack of listening. This can hurt, as we feel that the person has not bothered to listen to us, to hear our version of events.

There is a famous prayer attributed to Francis of Assisi. One of the lines says, 'O Divine Master, grant that I may not so much seek to be consoled as to console; to be understood as to understand; to be loved as to love.'

The writer of the prayer wanted to spend his time not justifying what he thought was right but trying to listen and learn from other people, to show them the value they should be given.

Words can mean different things to different people, as can tone of voice. We can misunderstand a person as being nice when they are actually being cruel. Look at this sentence: 'You're brilliant.' This can be a great compliment, but it can be said in a sarcastic way so that it actually means the opposite. We can work out the real meaning by hearing how the person speaks as well as by looking at the expression on their face. As we get to know people, we can tell when they are being kind or unpleasant.

While Paul was waiting in Athens, he was upset to see all the idols in the city. He went to the Jewish meeting place to speak to the Jews and to anyone who worshipped with them. Day after day he also spoke to everyone he met in the market. Some of them were Epicureans and some were Stoics, and they started arguing with him.

People were asking, 'What is this know-it-all trying to say?'

Some even said, 'Paul must be preaching about foreign gods! That's what he means when he talks about Jesus and about people rising from death.'

They brought Paul before a council called the Areopagus, and said, 'Tell us what your new teaching is all about. We have heard you say some strange things, and we want to know what you mean.'
ACTS 17:16–20

Reflection

One of the ways we can often misunderstand people is by reducing them to labels.

Read this advertisement, put together for the Embrace the Middle East charity. It is talking mainly about people in the Middle East, but it is true of other people and the way they feel.

The problem with me is, I'm complex.
You see me every day on TV, on the news.
You often forget about me.
People don't understand me.
Listen to me. I am a person, I am many people.
Embrace me.
Embrace the Middle East.

FEATURED IN *The Church Times at Greenbelt 2012*

☺ Questions and activities

- Why might we not understand something that someone has said to us? Draw a spider diagram to suggest some reasons why this happens.
- How can we make sure that we don't misunderstand another person? What do we need to do?
- Draw an image to show the idea of being misunderstood.
- When do you think that you have been misunderstood? How did it make you feel?
- Try to devise some rules with the rest of the class, to help you understand each other better, and write them up.
- Complete the activities on the 'Misunderstanding' wisdom sheet (see page 120).

Ideas for assembly themes

- Trying to understand other people—why empathy matters
- Being an effective listener—reflecting on having one mouth but two ears!
- Valuing and accepting difference

Wisdom sheet: Misunderstanding

Look at these ideas on misunderstanding. Choose one or more and comment on what the person is saying.

Where misunderstanding serves others as an advantage, one is helpless to make oneself understood.
LIONEL TRILLING

The world only goes round by misunderstanding.
CHARLES BAUDELAIRE

Is an intelligent human being likely to be much more than a large-scale manufacturer of misunderstanding?
PHILIP ROTH

It is by universal misunderstanding that all agree. For if, by ill luck, people understood each other, they would never agree.
CHARLES BAUDELAIRE

The single biggest problem with communication is the illusion that it has taken place.
GEORGE BERNARD SHAW

Finish your thoughts by completing these sentences:

- I think that misunderstandings happen because…
- The way to solve these misunderstandings is to…
- The last time I was misunderstood…

Reproduced with permission from *Emotionally Intelligent RE* by Cavan Wood (Barnabas in Schools, 2014)

Forgiveness: Jesus' teaching

Learning objectives

- All pupils will be able to explain the Christian ideas about forgiveness.
- Most pupils will be able to compare the Christian ideas about forgiveness with their own.
- Some pupils will be able to comment on whether it is always right to forgive.

Starter

- When you have done something wrong and ask someone for forgiveness, how do you know if they have forgiven you?

Introduction

As a group exercise, respond to each of these statements by moving around the classroom to one of three places labelled 'Yes', 'No' or 'Maybe'.

- I can forgive if someone calls me a name.
- I can forgive if someone has hit me.
- I can forgive if someone is rude about my mum or dad.
- I can forgive someone who breaks something that I own.
- I can forgive if someone is rude about my brothers or sisters.
- I could forgive a person who had harmed me in a war.
- No criminals can be forgiven.
- Murderers can never be forgiven.
- Racists can never be forgiven.
- I cannot forgive myself easily.

- I cannot forgive myself if I have hurt someone's feelings.
- I bear grudges easily.
- I can say 'sorry' when I know that I have been wrong.
- My parents have said 'sorry' to me when they have said or done something wrong.

The following passage tells us how Jesus answered a question about forgiveness from one of his disciples.

Peter came up to the Lord and asked, 'How many times should I forgive someone who does something wrong to me? Is seven times enough?'

Jesus answered: 'Not just seven times, but seventy-seven times!'
MATTHEW 18:21–22

At his own death, Jesus showed forgiveness to those who had put him to death on a cross.

Two criminals were led out to be put to death with Jesus. When the soldiers came to the place called 'The Skull', they nailed Jesus to a cross. They also nailed the two criminals to crosses, one on each side of Jesus.

Jesus said, 'Father, forgive these people! They don't know what they're doing.' …

One of the criminals hanging there also insulted Jesus by saying, 'Aren't you the Messiah? Save yourself and save us!'

But the other criminal told the first one off, 'Don't you fear God? Aren't you getting the same punishment as this man? We got what was coming to us, but he didn't do anything wrong.' Then he said to Jesus, 'Remember me when you come into power!'

Jesus replied, 'I promise that today you will be with me in paradise.'
LUKE 23:32–35, 39–43

Reflection

Did Jesus have the right to make this promise to the thief? Some would say that he did not.

Others believe that Jesus' own death helped to bring forgiveness to the world, that he 'paid the price of sin', as one hymn puts it. Forgiveness is right at the heart of the Christian religion.

Read this account of forgiveness. How do you respond to the Walker family's story?

Anthony Walker's family forgave the thugs who murdered their son and brother. Gee Walker, Anthony's mother, fought back tears as she overcame the urge to hate the two young people who killed her child. As a Christian, she said, she hoped the murderers would be able to forgive themselves.

She said, 'I can't hate. We're a forgiving family and it extended to outside, so it wasn't hard to forgive, because we don't just preach it, we practise it. I brought up my children in the Christian faith to love. I teach them to love, to respect themselves and others. What does bitterness do? It eats you up inside; it's a cancer. We don't want to serve a life sentence with the killers.'

Gee's daughter Dominique gave her strength throughout the worst moments of the trial. The 20-year-old had known one of her brother's killers at school. She forgave the killers. She said, 'Seventy times seven we must forgive. That's what we were taught; that's what the Bible said; that's what we have to do. It is hard, it is so hard, but you get through it. It eases the bitterness and the anger if you can wake up in the morning and think, "Forgive, forgive, and forgive".'

Anthony had been a Christian. His death touched many

people and encouraged them to stop the racism that had led to the crime.

☺ Questions and activities

- Draw an image to show the idea of forgiveness.
- 'Forgiving yourself when you do something wrong is even tougher than forgiving someone else.' What do you think? Give reasons for your answer, showing that you have thought about it from more than one point of view.
- If you had been Anthony Walker's mother or sister, do you think you could have forgiven his murderers?
- How do you feel when someone else forgives you when you have done something wrong to them?
- Complete the activities on the 'Forgiveness' wisdom sheet (see page 125).

Ideas for assembly themes

- How can we forgive?
- Positive change

Wisdom sheet: Forgiveness

Look at these ideas on forgiveness. Choose one or more and comment on what the person is saying.

Always forgive your enemies—nothing annoys them so much.
OSCAR WILDE

Forgiveness is the answer to the child's dream of a miracle by which what is broken is made whole again, what is soiled is made clean again.
DAG HAMMARSKJOLD

The weak can never forgive. Forgiveness is the attribute of the strong.
MAHATMA GANDHI

To forgive is to set a prisoner free and discover that the prisoner was you.
LEWIS B. SMEDES

One forgives to the degree that one loves.
FRANÇOIS DE LA ROCHEFOUCAULD

'I can forgive, but I cannot forget' is only another way of saying 'I cannot forgive.'
HENRY WARD BEECHER

Everyone says forgiveness is a lovely idea until they have something to forgive.
C.S. LEWIS

Finish your thoughts by completing these sentences:

* I think that forgiveness is...
* I find it easy/difficult to forgive another person because...

Reproduced with permission from *Emotionally Intelligent RE* by Cavan Wood (Barnabas in Schools, 2014)

+

Love: 1 Corinthians 13

Learning objectives

- All pupils will be able to explain the key ideas about the different types of love.
- Most pupils will be able to analyse these ideas, especially how they influence Christian behaviour in marriage and other relationships.
- Some pupils will be able to see the strengths and weaknesses of Christian teaching on love.

Starter

To have and to hold from this day forward; for better, for worse, for richer, for poorer, in sickness and in health, to love and to cherish, till death us do part.

- How realistic are these marriage vows today? What do you think? Give reasons for your answers.

Introduction

The group Foreigner had a song that said, 'I want to know what love is'. Love is a word that can have many meanings, and sometimes those meanings can be quite confusing. In his book *The Four Loves*, C.S. Lewis identified four types of love talked about in the Bible. He used these Greek words to explain them:

- **Storge:** the love we have for something like a food or a football team.
- **Philia:** the love we have for a friend or family member.

- **Eros:** romantic love.
- **Agape:** the selfless love that God has shown in the death of Jesus for people's sins, which Christians should try to copy.

Love is not something that can be earned: it is given. As the Beatles sang, 'Money can't buy you love'. They also realised that 'All you need is love'.

Now read this definition of love from Paul writing to the Corinthian church:

What if I could speak all languages of humans and of angels? If I did not love others, I would be nothing more than a noisy gong or a clanging cymbal. What if I could prophesy and understand all secrets and all knowledge? And what if I had faith that moved mountains? I would be nothing, unless I loved others. What if I gave away all that I owned and let myself be burnt alive? I would gain nothing, unless I loved others.

Love is kind and patient, never jealous, boastful, proud, or rude. Love isn't selfish or quick-tempered. It doesn't keep a record of wrongs that others do. Love rejoices in the truth, but not in evil. Love is always supportive, loyal, hopeful, and trusting. Love never fails!

Everyone who prophesies will stop, and unknown languages will no longer be spoken. All that we know will be forgotten. We don't know everything, and our prophecies are not complete. But what is perfect will someday appear, and what isn't perfect will then disappear.

When we were children, we thought and reasoned as children do. But when we grew up, we stopped our childish ways. Now all we can see of God is like a cloudy picture in a mirror. Later we will see him face to face. We don't know everything, but then we will, just as God completely understands us. For now there are faith, hope, and love. But of these three, the greatest is love.

1 CORINTHIANS 13:1–13

Reflection

How much like love are you? Can you put your name in the gaps?

* ...... is kind and patient.
* ...... is never jealous, boastful, proud or rude.
* ...... isn't selfish or quick-tempered.
* ...... doesn't keep a record of wrongs that others do.
* ...... rejoices in the truth, but not in evil.
* ...... is always supportive, loyal, hopeful and trusting.
* ...... never fails.

☺ Questions and activities

* Write a poem that explains your ideas about love. Each line should start with 'Love is' and should try to describe an emotion or an act that shows love.
* Draw a poster that explains three ideas about love.
* 'Love is a loser's game.' Is love a loser's game? What does this mean? Give reasons for your answer, showing that you have thought about it from more than one point of view.
* Write the marriage vows that you would be happy to take if you were to get married.
* Which of the four loves is the most difficult to live out?
* How important do you think it is to show faith, hope and love in your life?
* Complete the activities on the 'Love' wisdom sheet (see page 130).

Ideas for assembly themes

- Loving and accepting others
- Showing that we care for others
- Self-sacrifice

Wisdom sheet: Love

Look at these ideas on love. Choose one or more and comment on what the person is saying.

Affection is responsible for nine-tenths of whatever solid and durable happiness there is in our lives.
C.S. LEWIS

The hunger for love is much more difficult to remove than the hunger for bread.
MOTHER TERESA

Love takes up where knowledge leaves off.
THOMAS AQUINAS

I have decided to stick with love. Hate is too great a burden to bear.
MARTIN LUTHER KING, JR

Love is the greatest of all risks—the giving of myself.
JEAN VANIER

It is easier to love humanity as a whole than to love one's neighbour.
ERIC HOFFER

The supreme happiness of life is the conviction that we are loved.
VICTOR HUGO

Finish your thoughts by completing this sentence:

• I think that love is...

Humility: Philippians 2

Learning objectives

- All pupils will be able to explain the idea of humility.
- Most pupils will be able to explain Christian ideas about humility.
- Some pupils will be able to explain Christian and non-religious arguments for humility as well as exploring some of the positives and negatives of these beliefs.

Starter

- What is meant by the word 'humility'?
- Work with a partner to explain the idea and give an example of humility.

Introduction

The American country singer Mac Davis once released a record called 'It's hard to be humble when you are perfect in every way!' Very few people feel as confident as that title suggests, and I suspect that the singer was making a kind of joke. Yet some people say similar things and really mean it.

A man once came to a famous Christian speaker called Charles Spurgeon and said that he was perfect and that he had overcome all sin—all his negative emotions. Spurgeon smiled. He knew that the man was deluding himself and so he decided to do something to make him think again. He took a large jug of water and poured it over the man.

The man went red in the face and screamed at him, 'Why did you do that?'

'To show you that you are not perfect. You got angry because I poured water over you.'

The man realised that Spurgeon was right and that he was not the perfect person he had imagined. He had to accept that he was capable of making mistakes and was not as good as he thought he was.

We will never have a perfect world, but we might be able to make it better if we have a more realistic view of ourselves and others.

Read this passage from the Bible.

Christ encourages you, and his love comforts you. God's Spirit unites you, and you are concerned for others. Now make me completely happy! Live in harmony by showing love for each other. Be united in what you think, as if you were only one person. Don't be jealous or proud, but be humble and consider others more important than yourselves. Care about them as much as you care about yourselves and think the same way that Christ Jesus thought:

Christ was truly God.
But he did not try to remain equal with God.
Instead he gave up everything and became a slave,
when he became like one of us.

Christ was humble.
He obeyed God and even died on a cross.
Then God gave Christ the highest place
and honoured his name above all others.

So at the name of Jesus everyone will bow down,
those in heaven, on earth, and under the earth.
And to the glory of God the Father
everyone will openly agree, 'Jesus Christ is Lord!'
PHILIPPIANS 2:1–11

Reflection

Many people who study the Bible think that, in part of this passage from Philippians, Paul is quoting from an early Christian hymn. The hymn presents Christ as an image of what a person should be: Christians would say that he was God but also the perfect role model for all people. He was not big-headed but thought about the needs of others.

Dietrich Bonhoeffer said, 'Jesus was the man for others.' He was willing to die for others, to give his life for love. Could we do that?

Not to be big-headed is difficult enough. Choosing to put the needs of others above your own is difficult, if not impossible. Yet for Christians, the life of Jesus encourages them to do that, believing that this is the best way to live.

☺ Questions and activities

• Read and discuss this story about Jesus.

During the meal Jesus got up, removed his outer garment, and wrapped a towel around his waist. He put some water into a large bowl. Then he began washing his disciples' feet and drying them with the towel he was wearing.

But when he came to Simon Peter, that disciple asked, 'Lord, are you going to wash my feet?'

Jesus answered, 'You don't really know what I am doing, but later you will understand.'

'You will never wash my feet!' Peter replied.

'If I don't wash you,' Jesus told him, 'you don't really belong to me.'

Peter said, 'Lord, don't wash just my feet. Wash my hands and my head.'

JOHN 13:4–9

- Draw an image to show the idea of humility.
- How could you help someone today? What is stopping you from doing so?
- 'It is not a good idea to boast.' What do you think? Show that you have thought about your answer from more than one point of view.
- Who do you think of as role models? Why do you look up to these people?
- Complete the activities on the 'Humility' wisdom sheet (see page 135).

Ideas for assembly themes

- Having a right view of ourselves
- Valuing others
- Encouraging people, showing them their strengths and helping them to deal with their weaknesses
- Working in a team with others

Wisdom sheet: Humility

Look at these ideas on humility. Choose one or more and comment on what the person is saying.

Humility is not thinking less of yourself, it's thinking of yourself less.
RICK WARREN

Too much humility is pride.
GERMAN PROVERB

Humility is nothing else but a right judgement of ourselves.
WILLIAM LAW

Humility is really important because it keeps you fresh and new.
STEVEN TYLER

Without humility there can be no humanity.
JOHN BUCHAN

It is always the secure who are humble.
G.K. CHESTERTON

An able yet humble man is a jewel in the kingdom.
WILLIAM PENN

Finish your thoughts by completing these sentences:

- I think that humility is...
- On balance, I think that I am a humble/big-headed person because...

Reproduced with permission from *Emotionally Intelligent RE* by Cavan Wood (Barnabas in Schools, 2014)

✛

Afterword

In this book, I have attempted to connect the world of the emotions with the stories and insights of the Bible. For some, the Bible will always be a book that is the word of God. Others see it as the words of human beings. The truth, I think, is that it is about incarnation: we are confronted by the divine and the human in the story and teachings we encounter there, just as we see the human and divine in Jesus.

The great Victorian preacher C.H. Spurgeon was once asked if he would defend the Bible. He replied, 'Defend the Bible? That would be like defending a lion.' There is a power to help us see ourselves accurately in the Bible. Paul talked about how we usually see things as if they were a cloudy picture in a mirror (1 Corinthians 13:12): the images we see are distorted or not always clear. My belief is that emotional intelligence, coupled with the insights of the Bible into the timeless thoughts, feelings and actions of humanity, will help us to see ourselves more clearly.

C.S. Lewis wrote that he would like to help people discover a right image of God, of themselves, and of other people. I hope that this book will help people to do just that.

✣

Glossary

Acceptance: the act of taking or receiving; approval; assent to a belief.

Celebration: marking a special day or event, such as Christmas; making something known publicly; praising someone or something; performing a ceremony such as marriage.

Courage: the quality that helps a person to face difficulty, danger or pain bravely.

Curiosity: eagerness to learn or know; sometimes, the desire to find out information in a prying way.

Denial: stating that something said, believed or alleged is false; refusal to recognise or acknowledge something or someone (such as Peter's denial of Christ).

Despair: loss of hope, often causing acute sadness.

Doubt: uncertainty about a belief or a person; the thought that a claim is questionable or unlikely; hesitation to believe; a lack of trust.

Emotional intelligence: the different levels of understanding that people have when dealing with their emotions and the emotions of other people.

Fear: an upsetting emotion aroused by impending danger, evil, pain and so on, whether the threat is real or imaginary.

Fear of failure: the belief, sometimes irrational, that what we do will lead to failure.

Forgiveness: the act of letting go of a feeling of past wrong and resolving to be positive towards a person who has injured us.

Friendship: a relationship based on choice rather than blood, seeing the other person as of value and perhaps having a similar outlook or experience.

Grief: mental suffering or pain over suffering or loss; sharp sorrow; painful regret.

Guilt: a feeling of responsibility or regret for a crime or other wrong act, whether real or imagined.

Hope: the feeling that what is desired can be achieved or that events will turn out for the best.

Humility: the state of having a modest opinion or estimate of one's own importance; the opposite of arrogance.

Jealousy: the feeling of mental uneasiness from suspicion or envy of another's relationships or possessions.

Knowledge: an understanding of facts, truths or principles, gained by studying or investigating.

Love: a tender, passionate affection for another person; a feeling of warm personal attachment or deep affection for another, such as for a parent, child or friend; a sexual passion or desire.

Loyalty: faithfulness to a commitment or duties, such as in marriage or for your country.

Reproduced with permission from *Emotionally Intelligent RE* by Cavan Wood (Barnabas in Schools, 2014)

Misunderstanding: taking words or acts in a wrong sense; understanding wrongly, especially the intentions of another.

Moaning: complaining about something; expressing to others a feeling of pain.

Pride: a high, sometimes too high, opinion of our own dignity, importance or superiority.

Selfishness: the state of being devoted to or caring only about one's own needs or wants; concerned primarily with one's own interests, regardless of others and the effect on them.

Trust: confidence in the integrity, strength or ability of a person or thing; confident expectation of something; hope.

Wisdom: knowledge of what is true or right, coupled with an understanding of how to act rightly in a situation.

✣

Resources list

Books

- Daniel Goleman, *Emotional Intelligence* (Bloomsbury, 1996)
- Howard Gardner, *States of Mind* (Pan, 1994)
- *Aesop's Fables* (Penguin Classics, 1976)
- *Grimms' Fairy Tales* (many editions, first published 1812)
- Bob Hartman, *The Lion Storyteller Bible* (Lion Hudson, 2013)
- *The Poverty and Justice Bible* (Bible Society, 2013)
- Tony Castle (ed.), *The Hodder Book of Christian Quotations* (Hodder, 1982)

DVDs

- *Testament: The Bible in Animation* (Bible Society, 2009). Includes:
  - ✣ *Creation and the Flood*: the stories of Adam and Eve through to the story of Noah.
  - ✣ *Abraham*: the stories of Abraham and Isaac.
  - ✣ *Joseph*
  - ✣ *Moses*
  - ✣ *Ruth*

- *The Prince of Egypt* (DreamWorks, 2006): an excellent retelling of the story of Moses
- *The Miracle Maker* (Icon, 2007): a film about the life of Jesus that looks at several of the topics mentioned in this book
- *The Passion* (Acorn Media, 2009): series broadcast in 2008 by BBC1
- *Jesus of Nazareth* (ITV Studios, 2011): series broadcast in 1977 by ITV

Online resources

- www.biblegateway.com (various Bible translations to look up)
- www.youtube.com
- *Times Educational Supplement*: teacher resources

Music

- *Joseph and the Amazing Technicolor Dreamcoat* original cast album (Polydor, 2005)
- *The Prince of Egypt* (Polydor, 2002)

Magazines

- *Magnet* No. 98 (Summer 2012): contact www.ourmagnet.co.uk

Groups mentioned in this book

- Beachy Head chaplaincy: www.bhct.org.uk
- Cord and Tearfund (toilet twinning), PO Box 5050, Sherwood Business Park, Annesley, NG15 0DJ: www.toilettwinning.org
- Kimbilio: www.kimbiliocongo.org
- Langley House Trust, PO Box 181, Witney OX28 6WD
- Sojourners (co-founded by Jim Wallis): www.sojo.net
- USPG: www.weareus.org.uk

Also by Cavan Wood

Christianity: Key Beliefs and Traditions

An RE resource for teaching Christianity at Key Stage 2

Christianity: Key Beliefs and Traditions is an essential resource for teaching Christianity at Key Stage 2. It seeks to inform and equip RE teachers by looking at key theological ideas such as creation and salvation as well as at the life of Jesus and the growth of the church. Over 30 topics are covered, each including background information, classroom activities and learning objectives. The emphasis is not just on the history of Christianity but on the Christian faith as it is lived now and on evaluating its key ideas, linking themes to pupils' experience and understanding.

ISBN 978 0 85746 251 0   £7.99
Available direct from BRF: please visit www.barnabasinschools.org.uk

Enjoyed

this book?

Write a review—we'd love to hear what you think.
Email: reviews@brf.org.uk

Keep up to date—receive details of our new books as they happen.
Sign up for email news and select your interest groups at:
www.brfonline.org.uk/findoutmore/

Follow us on Twitter @brfonline

By post—to receive new title information by post (UK only), complete the form below and post to: BRF Mailing Lists, 15 The Chambers, Vineyard, Abingdon, Oxfordshire, OX14 3FE

Support your local bookshop
Ask about their new title information schemes.